The Saints' Treasury

Jeremiah Burroughs

Edited by Don Kistler

Soli Deo Gloria Publications
An imprint of Reformation Heritage Books
Grand Rapids, Michigan

Soli Deo Gloria Publications
An imprint of Reformation Heritage Books
3070 29th St. SE
Grand Rapids, MI 49512
616-977-0889
orders@heritagebooks.org
www.heritagebooks.org

The Saints' Treasury was first published in London during 1656.

Paperback reprint 2025

ISBN 979-8-88686-208-9

Printed in the United States of America
25 26 27 28 29 30/10 9 8 7 6 5 4 3 2 1

One always moves with fear and trepidation when attempting to edit the work of an author whose shoes he is unworthy to loose. However, in trying to fashion this collection of sermons into an acceptable format for the modern reader, it was necessary to make slight changes. Lengthy paragraphs have been shortened. Quotations marks were placed around quotes where there were none in the original. Spelling corrections have been made (*waie* has been changed to *way*). No changes have been made, however, in the Scripture quotations Burroughs used other than a few spelling corrections. The punctuation of the original Scripture references has been left intact.

While purists may take exception with any alteration of the manuscript, I am more concerned that the modern reader be able to benefit from this book without being obstructed by unnecessary difficulties. No substantive or doctrinal alterations have been made. I feel quite certain that if Mr. Burroughs were alive today, he would speak the language used today. Because of that, I have allowed myself these few minor changes.

Don Kistler
Soli Deo Gloria Publications

CONTENTS

DEDICATORY

To The Honorable Frances Rouse, Esq.
Speaker of the Parliament of the
Commonwealth of England and
Provost of Eaton College

Honored Sir,

If a heathen poet could say, "I shall live though I die," supposing his works to be immortal though he himself was mortal, upon how much better of an account may a prophet of the Lord say, "I shall not die, but live." This has respect both to his immortal soul, to which death is the gate of life, and the immortal travel of the soul, being conversant in the Word of the Lord that abides forever.

The works of the saints of God, in whom is the spirit of prophecy, not only live when they are dead, but are instrumental in the hand of grace, both to plant life where it is not and water it where it is, that it may spring forth more abundantly.

The chosen vessel of the Lord, by whose ministry He was pleased to give out the heavenly treasures laid up in these sermons, has some years since put off his earth and put on that inheritance of the saints in light, for which the Lord seemed to have fitted him early by his earnest and assiduous travail in fitting others. But though the vessel is broken, or rather is refined and translated to his Master's more immediate use, yet the treasures abide for the common enrichment of the saints. For spiritual treasures (like the loaves blessed

i

by our Saviour) multiply in their use and, when thousands have been enriched by them, still remain sufficient to enrich thousands.

To you, honored sir, this small but precious treasury is presented, not as though your own store was not already full. Who knows how many precious jewels (through the riches of Christ in you) you have richly set and polished to adorn the Bride, the Lamb's wife? Surely the Spirit of Christ seems to have chosen and sealed your spirit to celebrate His own nuptials in your mystical marriage and song of love.

Gold, besides its internal worth, receives an authentic impression from the image and superscription of the Prince. In honoring the Lord with the best part of our substance, a humble acknowledgment of His interest, both in the whole and ourselves (not any addition to His fulness) is intended. So this treasury is presented to the touch and test of your judgment, first as the standard of approving things that are excellent, and then as a humble testimony to how much he who presents this book owes you.

That the Lord would make you an ornament and defense to His saints and prosper His own pleasure in your hands is the prayer of, Honored Sir,

The most humble, and most
Obliged of your servants,

J.W.

To The Christian Reader

The author of the ensuing sermons has so abundantly approved himself to the church of God by his former labors, both in preaching and writing, that it would slight him to offer anything by way of commendation. His name is like a precious ointment, and so may it be as long as the sun and moon endure. These sermons will reveal themselves to be his genuine issue, the various features and proportions of his style (though styles differs as much as faces) are discernable here. Those who had the happiness to be conversant with him and listen to him are able to say, "So he opened his text, so he handled his doctrine, so he delivered his application." It is true, these fragments of his are under the prejudice of being posthumous works, but we suppose they are not inferior to the rest of his works. Though they are born out of due time, and though they are fragments, they are to be esteemed. These sermons are to be prized for their own worth and intrinsical excellence, whoever the author was, and this author is to be honored for his real worth, whatever he is the author of.

We shall add also, for your encouragement, that these sermons have been very happily taken by the pen of a ready writer, Mr. Farthing, now a teacher of shorthand writing, one who has given ample testimony of his great skill and dexterity in writing shorthand. We think we may say that there are not many words delivered by the author that have been left out. However, we are confident that there is nothing essential preached by him that, by the care and faithfulness of the scribe, is not here presented to your view.

The desire of the publishers is that the name of this worthy man of God may be kept in your honor, that you may transfer these things to your own use and express them in your life, that what was spoken to some may be common to all, that what was accepted by them who heard it may be received and improved by those that read it. This is all we have to communicate to you. It would be an injury to detain you longer from the reverend author. We only commend you to the grace of God which is able to make you abound in every good work, and bid you farewell.

James Nalton	Matthew Poole
William Cooper	Allen Geare
Thomas Jacomb	Ralph Venning

September 29, 1653

IMPRIMATUR,

Edmund Calamy

SERMON 1
"Who is like unto Thee, O Lord, amongst the gods!
Who is like unto Thee, glorious in holiness,
fearful in praises, doing wonders!"
(Exodus 15:11)

This Scripture is this day fulfilled in our ears and before our eyes. That which God has already begun to do for this kingdom and the neighboring churches, shows us that there is none like the Lord, *who is glorious in holiness, fearful in praises, doing wonders.*

The words, though they are in the middle of a song, are a kind of an epiphonema, a conclusion which is usually at the end, but the spirit of Moses, admiring and blessing God for the great things He had done for His people, does not wait for the end but breaks forth in the very middle with the applause of the glory of God, *Who is like unto Thee, O Lord, amongst the gods, who is like unto Thee, glorious in holiness, fearful in praises, doing wonders!* You see, then, that the words are a part of Moses' song, occasioned upon the goodness of God in delivering His people from Egypt and carrying them through the Red Sea.

This is the most ancient song in the world. It is the first in Scripture, and we know of no author before Moses. Those who were skillful in poetry came many hundreds of years after Moses. It is a spiritual and a most excellent song. The style is full of elegance, the matter is of great variety. It is eucharistical, triumphant, prophetical, and it is a pity we do not have such an excellent song as this turned into meter to be sung in our congregations. It is a most delightful song, and therefore observe that when God promised a mercy to His people, in which they should rejoice exceedingly, He refers to this song, Hosea 2:15, *And I will give her vineyards from thence, and the valley of Achor for a door of hope, and she shall sing there as in the days of her youth, and as in the day when she came out of the land of Egypt.*

When God intended any great mercy to His people, He wanted them to sing this song of Moses. So then, if God is in a way of mercy, if He is opening a door of hope to us, you can see how timely the song is. It is a symbolic song, as the deliverance of God's people out of Egypt is a type of the deliverance of God's people from the bondage of Antichrist. Therefore, it is observable that this song is to be sung again when the people of God are delivered from the Antichrist. In Rev. 15:1-2, you see God's judgments upon Antichrist. In verse 3 it is said *they sing the song of Moses the servant of God, and the song of the Lamb, saying 'Great and marvelous are Thy works, God almighty; just and true are Thy ways, thou King of Saints.'* By this you may see that God would show us that the bondage under Antichrist is like the bondage in Egypt, and therefore Rome is called Egypt in Revelation because, when we shall be delivered from Antichristian bondage under Antichrist. It is good for us to acquaint ourselves with this song because it is that which will be sung over again when the bondage of Antichrist is removed. It is a miraculous song, according to the opinion of Austin. He brings in this song as one of the miracles, that is, that God, at the same time by the Spirit, inspired all the people of Israel to sing one and the same song together, and therefore it was miraculously true if it had been so, but the Scripture is not clear in that.

But we leave the generals and come to the words which are, as it were, a recapitulation of all, containing the substance of all, as if he had said, "I have spoken of many particulars that God does for his people...but there is none like unto the Lord, who is glorious in holiness, fearful in praises, doing wonders." There are four things wherein the name of God is advanced here. First, there is none like the Lord; secondly, glorious in holiness; thirdly, fearful in praises; and fourthly, doing wonders.

I confess that when my thoughts first came to speak upon this text, I intended only the one particular, the opening of that title of God, "fearful in praises." We do not find any such title in all the book of God that I know of, except in this one place. But because I saw that there was much of God in the two former ones, I thought it useful to show you what there is of God in them and was unwilling to pass them by.

For the first then, *Who is like to Thee, O Lord, amongst the gods, who is like to Thee, glorious in holiness, who is like to Thee?* This, you see, is put in the form of interrogation. Interrogations in Scripture are especially brought in two ways: first, by way of admiration; secondly, by way of negation. Sometimes it is by way of admiration, Isaiah 63:1, *Who is this that cometh from Edom with dyed garments from Bazrah!* We might name many others by way of admiration. There are hundreds of examples of the way of negation. We are to understand both of these in this text. First, by way of admiration, *Who is like unto Thee, O Lord, amongst the gods,* and so on. Moses and the people, being struck with astonishment at the glory of God now manifested by the great works He had done, admire Him and say, *Who is like unto Thee, O Lord?* By way of negation, *Who is like unto Thee, O Lord?* That is, there is none like Thee. That is the first expression of the glory of God, the lifting up of the name of God above all things whatever, *there is none like God.*

God so glories in this expression of His glory, that there is none like Him. We see this often in Scripture, I Chron. 17:20, *O Lord, there is none like Thee, neither is there any God besides Thee, according to all that we have heard with our ears.* So also Psalm 86:8, *Among the gods there is none like unto Thee, O Lord.* And Psalm 89:6, *For who in heaven can be compared unto the Lord? Who among the sons of the mighty can be likened unto the Lord?* We might name various other places where God glories greatly in the expression of His glory. The people of God have gloried much in it, and there is great cause that they should do so.

It is said of the godly Maccabees that at first, by reason, their name was an offense, meeting with this sentence, "Who is like unto Thee, O Lord, amongst the gods?" Being quite taken with it, they wrote the first

Hebrew letter of every word in this sentence in their banners of war, and carried them with them. Upon this ground they were called the Maccabees, glorying in this title of God, "Who is like unto Thee?"

Upon this same ground the Holy Ghost concludes that all should honor and glorify God, because there is none like Him. *Among the gods there is none like unto Thee, O Lord, neither are there any works like unto Thy works*, Psalm 86:8. Mark what follows in verses 9-12, *All nations whom Thou hast made, shall come and worship before Thee, O Lord, and shall glorify Thy name; for Thou art great and doest wondrous things, for Thou art God alone; teach me Thy ways, O Lord, I will walk in Thy truth; unite my heart to fear Thy name; I will praise Thee, O Lord my God, with all my heart, and I will glorify Thy name forevermore.* Thus you see how the holy prophet was taken with this expression of God, that there is none like Him, therefore, *teach me Thy way, O Lord, I will walk in Thy truth.*

There is none like unto the Lord amongst the Gods. It might as well be translated "among the mighties." God is lifted up here not only among the heathen gods, so that there is none like Him among them, but He is also lifted up above whatever has any excellency in it. "There is none like Thee among the mighties." Whoever is mighty and great, yet God is infinitely above all. It would take up too much of our time if we were to speak at length to show you something of the glory of God in this, how He is above all things and that there is none like Him. I will, therefore, only name a few passages, apply this particular, and move on to the second.

There is none like God, first, in that whatever is in God is God Himself. This is a property of God. There is no creature who has any excellency in it that reaches to this excellency, that whatever is in that creature is the being of it, all creatures being made up of several things. Whatever is in God is God Himself. Again, there is a universal goodness in God and there is none like Him in that. One creature has one good in it and another another, but God has all good in Him. There is all excellency and beauty in God in an eminent manner, there is none like Him in that. All beings are just one excellency in God, but we apprehend God in several excellencies, one attribute shining through one creature and another through another, yet all are united in God. And all that is in Him is originally in Him, He is of Himself and from Himself and for Himself. Then none can communicate Himself as God can, none can inflict evil or convey good as God can.

It is peculiar to God to communicate as much of Himself as He will, which no creature can do. Though the creature has only little, some drops of goodness in comparison to the infinite ocean that is in God, yet the creature cannot communicate those drops as he wills. It is the propriety of God alone to communicate His goodness as He wills. And not only so, but He can make the creature to which He communicates His goodness to be as sensible of His goodness as He pleases, which none else can do. Though one creature can communicate good to another, it cannot make that creature as sensible of that good as it wills, which God can do.

And so in inflicting evil, there is none like the Lord in that. The Lord is able to let out all evil, to bring all evil at once, which none else can do. He is able to make the creature upon whom He inflicts an evil to be as sensible of that evil as He wills. One can hurt another but he cannot make him as sensible of that hurt as he pleases, but this God can do. As He can bring all evil together, so He is able to make the creature as sensible of all as He wills, and God challenges this as His own propriety, that He alone can do good and He alone can do evil and therefore there is none like Him.

As a result it follows, then, that there is none to be worshipped as the Lord. There is none to be honored as the Lord. The heathen gods, because they only communicated some particular good, demanded only particular service. External worship, and worship in some particulars, would serve the heathen gods and they were satisfied with it and required no more. There was a reason for it, because they could not challenge to themselves a communication of a universal good, for one god was for one particular good and another for another particular good. Therefore they had only particular worship suitable to them, but there is none like the Lord. He demands a universal worship and obedience, *Thou shalt worship the Lord thy God with all thy heart, and soul, and strength.* So that there is none like Him in the excellency of His nature and in the way of communicating Himself unto His creature.

Now this which I have spoken is exceedingly useful in the whole course of our lives in ordering our ways and thoughts toward God. Consider how useful it is. It should be our care in beholding any beauty, any good or excellency in the creature, to keep still in our thoughts and hearts the infinite distance there is between God and the creature. The lack of this is the cause of almost all the evil there is in the world, and the true apprehension of this is a special means to enable us to glorify God as God. So I say, when you behold any excellency, beauty, or comeliness in a creature and taste any sweetness in it, be sure you then keep in your heart the sense of this truth, that though there is some sweetness here, yet God is infinitely above the creature, and there is an infinite disproportion between that good, beauty, and excellency that is in these creatures and God Himself. God gives us permission to let our hearts out on, and to take the comfort of, the creature when we see a beauty and excellency in it. That is because it is His image upon the creature and it is God's excellency that is there. A spiritual heart has more freedom to let itself out to the comforts of the creature than any in the world, because he can meet with and taste God there. But though God gives us permission to do this, yet it is so that evermore we will be sure to reserve our hearts to God, to be aware of the infinite excellency that is in God above any creature and, if we are not careful, we will soon fall off from glorifying God as God and our hearts will stick to the creature.

This has been the ground of all the outward and spiritual idolatry in the world. Outward idolatry arose thusly: men first seeing some excellency and worth in the creature (as the sun, moon, and stars) acknowledged God as being above them and that these were but creatures. There was more excellency in God than in any of these, but at last coming to look upon the creature too much, and being taken with the excellency they saw there, their hearts stuck on the creature. They lost the apprehension of the infinite excellency of God above the creature and so fell from God and worshipped them who were not gods.

Spiritual idolatry has to do with those who commit idolatry with riches or any creature. Come to them and say, "How do you apprehend the comforts of the creature? Is there not infinitely more in God than there is in the creature?"

"Yes," they will say, "but by letting our hearts out upon the creature and by gazing upon the beauty of the creature, we begin at length to lose the power of this understanding that was on our hearts and so commit spiritual idolatry with the creature." Therefore it must be our care to keep fresh and unbroken our apprehension and sense of that infinite distance that there is between God and all the comforts of the creature.

As long as you keep your apprehensions fresh and strong here, there is no danger and you do not sin in letting out yourself to the creature if it has not abated your apprehension of the infinite disproportion between God and the creatures. Therefore now, seeing that there is an infinite, overwhelming height of excellency in God above all creatures, there should be similar thoughts in our hearts toward God and the creature. As there is an infinite distance between the excellency of God and the excellency of all creatures, so there ought to be a kind of infiniteness in the distance and disproportion between that esteem, delight, and dependence we have in and upon the creature and that which we have in and upon God. Therefore, you should not satisfy yourselves in that you acknowledge God above the creature, for all will do so. But you are to find in your souls such a disproportion between your esteem, joy, and desire for the creature and that which you have for God is something like the distance there is between God and the creature. Now the distance is infinite between God and the creature. Therefore, there should be a kind of infiniteness in the distance between your esteem of, and the workings of your hearts and endeavors after, the creature and the esteem and workings of your hearts and souls which you have towards God. This is to glorify God as God. This is the soul worship we owe to God in the world. This is the true sanctifying of the name of God when this comes practically upon our hearts.

Secondly, if there is none like God, then it follows that there are none like the people of God, for as a man's God is, so is he. Whatever god a man chooses, he is as his god is. If a covetous man makes riches his god, he is so to be judged, and so a voluptuous man or a heathen. Now if the saints of God have chosen this

God to be their God, and if there is none like Him, then it must follow that there are no people like God's people.   Mark how the Holy Ghost makes this inference in various Scriptures. Deut.33:26 and 29, *There is none like unto the God of Jeshurun, who rideth upon the heaven, in thy help and in His excellency in the sky.* What is the logical conclusion of the Holy Ghost? *Happy art thou, O Israel, who is like to thee, O people saved by the Lord.* So that you see according to the glory of God in any particular, there is a reflection of it upon the saints of God, and this is the wonderful excellency of God's saints, to have the reflection of God upon them. Happy are they who have God to be their God. If God is so excellent, so are they! If God is above all and there is none like Him, so are they above all and there are none like them!

You have the same inference of the Holy Ghost in II Samuel 7:22-23, *Wherefore Thou art great, O Lord God, for there is none like Thee, neither is there any God besides Thee; according to all that we have heard with our ears.* Mark what follows, *and what one nation in the earth is like Thy people, even like Israel?* So that there are none like the people of God, and it must follow from this, for they are as their God is. Therefore Moses says, speaking of the people of God in Exodus 33:16, *So shall we be separated, I and Thy people, from all the people that are upon the earth.* That is how you read it in your Bibles, but the word in the original signifies "wonderfully separated." God's people are wonderfully separated from the world. As

God is wonderfully high above all creatures, so are His people. Therefore in Numbers 27:9 it is said that *God's people shall dwell alone, and shall not be reckoned among the nations*. Why? Because they are the people of God, and the people of that God who has none like Him, and therefore there are none like them. That is the consolation of the saints of God.

Thirdly, it follows from this that it should be our care that none should do for their gods as we do for ours. For if there is none like our God, then it is a shame that any who choose other gods should do for them that which is above what we do for our God. As for idolaters, there is none like our God. Certainly all the idolaters in the world do not have a god as we have, their rock is not as our Rock. What a shame it would be, then, if we should do no more for our God than they do for theirs. Yea, we should labor to do that for our God which will come up to the level of excellency we perceive to be in Him.

Will you see what idolaters do for their gods? First, observe the earnestness of the spirits of idolaters after their gods. Their hearts are enflamed with their idols. So we have in Isaiah 57:5, ...*enflaming yourselves with idols under every green tree*. Their hearts were enflamed after their idol gods which are not like our God! Oh how, then, should our hearts be enflamed after our God! Should we content ourselves with, and rest satisfied in, cold and dead services to our God? How much strength should that exhortation of the Apostle have upon us in Romans 12:11, *Be fervent in spirit, serving the Lord.* It is the Lord we serve, it is our God, the great and glorious God, and therefore we should be fervent in spirit, serving Him.

Secondly, the Scripture says that idolaters, those who worship false gods, are mad upon their idols, Jer.50:38. The people of God, then, should have their hearts run after God so that those who are carnal and not able to judge should look upon them as madmen, and indeed they are so. Whenever the hearts of the saints are fully after God they are looked upon as madmen. St.Paul was counted a madman by Festus, Acts 26:24, and we should not be afraid of the reproaches of the world in this way, though they despise us and think of us as base, vile, and out of our wits. Idolaters are mad upon their idols. Therefore, if there is anything God calls for at our hands, though the world accounts it as madness, yet our hearts must work after God in it. It is a shame that any men's hearts should be more for their gods than our hearts are for ours, because there is none like our God.

Thirdly, the earnestness of the hearts of idolaters after their idol gods appears from Jer.8:1-2, *At that time saith the Lord, They shall bring out the bones of the Kings of Judah, and they shall spread them before the sun, and the moon, and all the host of heaven, whom they have loved, and whom they have served, and after whom they have walked, and whom they have sought, and whom they have worshipped: they shall not be gathered, nor be buried.* I have often thought of this Scripture, it is exceedingly remarkable. I do not know one Scripture in all the book of God that has as many expressions to show the strength of the hearts of God's people after God as this one, which shows the strength of idolaters after their idols. *And they shall spread them before the sun, and the moon, and all the hosts of heaven....* Mark it: (1) whom they have loved; (2) whom they have served; (3) after whom they have walked; (4) whom they have sought; (5) whom they have worshipped, and all in so few words. Thus their hearts were after their idol gods. How much more, then, ought it to be said of us concerning our God, whom we have loved, and whom we have served, and after whom we have walked, and whom we have sought, and whom we have worshipped.

Observe how the Scripture sets out the spirits of men after their idol gods with regard to the cost they are willing to bestow upon them. Isaiah 46:6 says, *They shall lavish gold out of the bag, and weigh silver in the balance, and hire a goldsmith, and he maketh it a god.* They do not care what it costs to worship their idols. Oh, what a shame would it be if we should not be willing to part with much of our estates for the true worship of the true God. Though we might lose our estates, if we can serve God better and in a purer way, we should be content, for idolaters will lavish gold out of the bag on their idols. Now there is none like our God, therefore it is a shame that they should do more for their gods than we do for ours.

And then what are idolaters willing to suffer for their gods? In I Kings 18:28, the priests of Baal cut themselves with knives and lances until the blood gushed out to show their respect to their idols. Let us then be willing to suffer anything that God calls us to. And how constant they were to their idols. Therefore God says in Jer.2:10-11, *Consider diligently and see if there be such a thing: hath a nation changed their gods which are yet no gods? But my people have changed their glory for that which doth not profit.* How badly God takes this that idolaters will not change their gods which are infinitely below Him, and yet His people change their God who is infinitely above them!

Again, let us take heed lest there be any found who have their hearts set more upon their lusts than we are upon God. Take all the excellencies in the world and they are infinitely below God. How much more, then, is a lust below God? For what is a lust in comparison of all creatures in heaven and earth? Yet how are men's hearts set upon their lusts? Yea, how has your own heart been set upon wicked lusts before this? Then think to yourself what an infinitely unreasonable thing it is that the heart of any man in the world, or your own heart, should be set more upon a base lust than upon the living, eternal, and infinite God. It is said of Ahab that he sold himself to work wickedness, I Kings 21:20. Then you be willing to sell yourself to God, to give up yourself to God. Ecc.8:11 says that *the hearts of the sons of men are set, and fully set to do evil.* Do not content yourself with some faint wishes and desires after God, but let your heart be set, and fully set, for God. In Micah 7:3 it is said ...*they do evil with both hands earnestly*. Mark it. They do evil, and they do evil earnestly, and they do evil earnestly with both hands. Now then, for shame! Do not be sluggish in doing service for your God. Do that which is good, and do it with both your hands, and do it earnestly with all your heart.

We have one more notable Scripture that shows how the hearts of men are set upon that which is evil. Prov.19:28 says, *The mouth of the wicked devoureth iniquity*. It is an elegant expression of the Holy Ghost. It is a metaphor taken from the practice of brute creatures. Take a beast that has been kept from drink a long time and is exceedingly thirsty. If you bring it to the water, it will thrust its head into the water as if it would devour the whole river and never be satisfied. That is the meaning of this phrase, "the mouth of the wicked devoureth iniquity." When he comes to his sin, he is as greedy of it as the beast that has been kept from water is greedy of water. Oh how our hearts should be infinitely more greedy after God and His service than wicked men are, or can be, after the service of their lusts.

To conclude all this, you have Exodus 30, verse 34 to the end. There was a perfume there to be made by the composition of the chemist, but there was this charge given, ...*as for the perfume which thou shalt make, you shall not make to yourselves, according to the composition thereof, it shall be unto thee holy for the Lord*. So I conclude this point: there is none like God, He is above all. When your hearts, therefore, are in any good frame towards God, perfumed and lifted up towards God, take heed that they are not lifted up towards any creature in the same manner as they are towards God, for your service to God must be suitable to the nature of God. Now there is none like God, therefore there should be no service tendered to any as it is tendered to God. This much for the first thing whereby the name of God is advance here, *Who is like unto Thee, O Lord, among the gods!*

We now come to the second, "glorious in holiness." The word translated here as "glorious" as well signifies "magnificent" or "noble," and so it is used in many places, *Thou art magnificent and noble in Thy holiness.* Brethren, it is the greatest magnificence, the greatest nobility and height of spirit that can be, to be holy. God Himself is a magnificent God and He is ennobled by His holiness. This sets out the excellency of holiness.

"Glorious in holiness" is rendered by some as "glorious in holy things," that is, glorious in His holy angels, glorious in His holy saints, glorious in His holy Word, glorious in His holy ordinances, glorious in His holy worship. God, indeed, is very glorious in His angels, in His saints, in His Word, in His worship, and in His ordinances, but we will take the words as you have them here, "glorious in holiness."

For the explication of the glory of God in this title, there are these three things to be done: first, to show you a little what holiness in God is; secondly, I shall open to you how God is said to be glorious in holiness;

and then thirdly, I shall show you why God has this title given to Him, why He is said to be glorious in holiness rather than glorious in power, for it was an act of power that God put forth in the destruction of the Egyptians and deliverance of His people.

First, what is holiness in God? We understand this, as we do most things about God, by way of negation: by what it is not rather than by what it is. We used to say that God's holiness is that whereby His nature is free from all kinds of mixture, from the least soil and filth of sin. Therefore, God is called light because light is so pure a creature, and so free from any mixture of pollution that it can be among filthy things without being defiled itself. So God can work with sin itself without any defilement of His nature.

If you would know what the holiness of God is from a positive position, I would describe it to you thusly: it is the infinite rectitude and perfection of the will of God especially whereby He wills and works all things suitable to the infinite excellency of His own being. The excellency of God is the highest and, therefore, the rule of all excellency, and the will of God, being always suitable to His own infinite excellency and unable to vary in the least from it, is the rule of all holiness.

Let us consider it a little by looking into the holiness of the creature, and by that we shall see something of the holiness of God, for as we cannot see the glory of the sun by looking directly on it (being too bright an object for us, so that we behold its glory by the reflection of the beams in the water), so the holiness of God is too bright to be beheld in itself. We cannot behold the infinite purity and holiness of God immediately, but by looking upon the creature which is, as it were, the reflection of God's holiness upon it, a ray and beam of it, we may come to see something of the holiness of God.

The holiness of a creature is the separation of it from common things to a holy use, or the dedication of a creature in some immediate manner to God for the lifting up of His name. The holiness of the saints is the separation of their spirits from all common things to God as the highest and last end. When they are able to work to God as the utmost end and to will what they do in order to God as the last end, and so as is suitable to God as the highest end, that is the holiness of their wills.

So it is in God's holiness. God's holiness is a dedication, as it were, of God to Himself; that is, God, being of and from Himself and having Himself as His own last end, gives up Himself to Himself and wills Himself as the highest and utmost end, and so wills all things in order to Himself as the last and highest end. This is the holiness of God, and the image of this holiness is that stamp and work of grace that is upon the creature. When the creature is enabled to will God as the highest end and all things in subordination to Him, the creature is then said to be holy because it has a stamp of God upon it. This is God's holiness.

But "glorious in holiness?" How is God "glorious

in holiness?" God is glorious in all His attributes and works, and, the truth is, there is not one thing in God more glorious than another, every attribute of God being in itself equally glorious. But in regard to manifestation, and according to our apprehension, one thing appears more glorious than another and God is pleased to speak to us according to our apprehensions. Therefore you may see how the saints especially glory in God as a holy God. Looking upon Him as a holy God, they greatly rejoice and glory in Him. Therefore the Psalmist says, Ps.99:3, *Let them praise Thy great and terrible name, for it is holy,* and verse 5, *Exalt ye the Lord our God, and worship at His footstool, for He is holy.* And later in verse 9, *Exalt the Lord our God, and worship at His holy hill, for the Lord our God is holy.*

Thus the people of God look upon God in His holiness as the special ground of His praise and exaltation. Yea, the angels in heaven look upon God in His holiness and especially exalt Him because of this, Isaiah 6:3. The cherubim and seraphim cry three times, *Holy, holy, holy is the Lord of hosts.* You will never find any of God's attributes mentioned in this way three times together. It is true, though, that God is infinite in power and wisdom as well as in holiness, yet you never find in Scripture that God is said to be wise, wise wise, or almighty, almighty, almighty, but holy, holy, holy, three times together. And as the angels of heaven adore God especially for His holiness, so the church of God, Rev.4:8, cries out, *Holy, holy,*

holy, Lord God almighty, showing the blessed condition of the church of God when it shall be hereafter more sanctified. God shall dwell among them and then they shall exceedingly adore God's holiness above any other attribute.

Yea, God Himself seems to glory in His holiness above any other attribute. Therefore, when God would lift Himself up in His glory and give you the highest expression of Himself, He does it in this: that He is holy. Isaiah 57:15, *For thus saith the high and lofty One that inhabiteth eternity, whose name is holy.* When God would lift Himself up, it is in this: *whose name is holy.* So when God would swear by Himself, Amos 4:2, He swears by His holiness. Now as the Scripture says that when God could swear by nothing greater He swore by Himself, so I say that when God could swear by no excellency above this, He swears by His holiness.

God glories in heaven itself as the inhabitation of His holiness. Heaven is the habitation of God's glory. There God lets His glory out fully, but what is that glory? Why, the top of all is the holiness of God, Is.63:15, *Look down from heaven and behold from the habitation of Thy holiness and Thy glory.* Yea, the throne of God is God's holiness, Psalm 47:8, *God sitteth upon the throne of His holiness.* You know that kings on their thrones are exalted and lifted up, so God is lifted up on the throne of His holiness. Solomon made himself a throne of ivory and overlaid it with the best gold, I Kings 10:18, but the throne of God is a throne of holiness, a throne of bright, shining holiness.

When God rejoices in His people, He does it as they are a holy people, Deut.7:6, *For thou art a holy people unto the Lord thy God: the Lord thy God hath chosen thee to be a peculiar people unto Himself above all the people that are upon the face of the earth.* Further, you find that this attribute of holiness is more especially attributed to the third person of the Trinity. God the Father is a holy God, the Son is the holy One of God, but the Holy Ghost has His name from holiness. It is very observable that all three persons demand an equal share in the working of holiness in the creature, being such a part of God's glory that all three persons work it wherever it is.

The Father is a Sanctifier. Jude speaks of the work of sanctification wrought by God the Father in the first verse of his epistle, *To them that are sanctified by God the Father.* The Son, Eph.5:25-26, *Husbands, love your wives, even as Christ also loved the church and gave Himself for it, that He might sanctify and cleanse it with the washing of water by the Word.* Christ gives Himself for His church. To what end? Not only that He might bring it to heaven, but that He might sanctify it also. Then the Spirit of God, I Cor.6:11, *And such were some of you, but ye are washed, but ye are sanctified, but ye are justified, in the name of the Lord Jesus, and by the Spirit of our God.* So that all three persons come in for a share in this work. This is the glorious work of the Father, Son, and Holy Ghost.

But to further demonstrate it, holiness must be the

glory of God because it is the highest perfection and rectitude of an intelligent free agent. An intelligent free agent is the highest being of all, and holiness is the rectitude of that being and therefore must be glorious. Hence it is that grace is called God's image because it is that which represents God in His highest excellency. An image of something is that which sets forth the excellency of it. If it only does it in a common and general way, it is not an image. In Scripture, holiness is called the beauty of God, Psalm 27:4, *One thing I have desired of the Lord, that I will seek after, that I may dwell in the house of the Lord all the days of my life, to behold the beauty of the Lord, and to enquire in His temple.* Now what is God's beauty but the beauty of holiness? The holiness of God which appears in His ordinances and His worship is the luster and beauty of the infinite God of glory. In Psalm 110:3 the ordinances are called the beauty of holiness, *Thy people shall be willing in the day of Thy power of the beauties of holiness.*

Yea, seeds of holiness, even the very image of it in the creature is called the glory of God, Rom.3:23, *All have sinned and come short of the glory of God.* The very beginning of the work of holiness in the hearts of saints is called the glory of God, much more, then, the infinite holiness of God's own nature. Further, it is holiness that puts a luster upon all the other attributes of God and makes them glorious and honorable. Psalm 111:9, *Holy and reverend is His name.* This name of God is therefore worthy of reverence because it is holy.

So take all the height of excellencies that are in God. If they are such as you can conceive them separated from His holiness, they do not make His name worthy of reverence. This shows how infinitely it concerns us to labor after holiness. If all the excellencies of God cannot make His name worthy of reverence, being separated from holiness, then let the creature have what excellency it will for parts, for estate, for dignity and honor in the world. Take away holiness and you cannot say reverend is His name, but it is *holy and reverend is His name.* It is said of God that His name is reverend because it is holy.

God's name is glorious because of holiness, because it is the special end of all His works to advance holiness. When an artist draws something, he shows art in the beginning, but when he comes to the end he shows the excellency of his workmanship. It is so with God. God will be honored in all His works of creation and providence, but now He comes to the height and zenith of all, and it is that He might be honored as a holy God and that He might have a holy people to honor Him here and to all eternity. Holiness is that at which God aimed in creating heaven and earth. It is that at which God aims in all the ways of His providence. It is the great business for which the Son of God came into the world: that He might redeem to Himself a people to serve Him in holiness. It is the end of the great counsel of God from all eternity: that He might manifest the beauty of His own holiness in those two great attributes, mercy and justice. These are the branches of His holiness. That He might make them shine to all eternity, this is that at which God aims. Therefore holiness must be the glory of God's name.

But what is the reason this title is given to God in the song of Moses, "glorious in holiness?" The reason is to show that the infinite excellency of God's power is such that it is without any mixture of the least evil in exercising it. Here was an act of mighty power put forth, and God was infinitely holy in this act of power. It is otherwise with men (observe the difference between God and men). It is a very hard thing for a man to do great things and to manifest great power without a mixture of evil. When water runs shallow it may run clearly, but once the waters rise and overflow, they run muddy. Usually a great deal of filth comes in with great streams. We do not manifest our uncleanness in common and ordinary works, but when we aim to do great things. Seldom do we not manifest a great deal of filthiness, but it is otherwise with God. God is great in power and, in that, keeps the glory of His holiness. And God manifested here the greatness of His wrath upon His enemies and the glory of His holiness, too.

It's a very hard thing for men to do this. Let men have their anger stirred a little and how much filth they reveal! How many are there who are exceedingly meek and loving while they are pleased, but let anything stir their passion and what a great deal of filth appears. Like a pond that is full of mud at the bottom and clear at the top, stir it a little and it is nothing but filth. A father or a mother cannot be displeased with a child or correct it without having an abundance of corruption come upon their anger, nor can a governor with his servant. Who can execute justice upon others without having much of self, self-ends, and self-interest? But here is the glory of God, that when He manifests His wrath, though it is sore wrath, He is still glorious in holiness in great wrath.

He is infinitely powerful in His wrath and in the execution of His judgments, and yet infinite in holiness, too. Therefore the vials of God's wrath are said to be made of gold, which is the purest metal. So is God in the executing of His judgments. Oh, let us labor to imitate God in this. You who have a passionate spirit and are easily provoked and reveal an abundance of filthiness, how unlike God you are. Though you are displeased with that which is sinful and may correct your children and your servants, be sure to keep that which is the beauty of all in correcting others, and that is holiness.

This title is given to God because, in this great work of His, He manifested His faithfulness by fulfilling His promises to His people. God made many promises to His people for their preservation and deliverance, and God fulfilled these promises. Now God's faithfulness is a branch of His holiness. Therefore, because He manifested His faithfulness in this work, Moses and the other people extol His name by this great title, "glorious in holiness." It is of great use to us that God's faithfulness is a branch of His holiness. If you compare two Scriptures, you will find it so. Isaiah 55:3 is one where God says, *I will make an everlasting covenant with you, even the sure mercies of David.* And this Scripture is quoted in Acts 13:34, *I will give you the sure mercies of David.* That is how we read it, but in the original it is "the holy and faithful things of David." So that when God comes to show mercy according to His Word, He manifests the glory of His holiness, and it is of admirable use to God's people to strengthen their faith.

You have heard that the glory of God is His holiness. Now one part of this holiness is His faithfulness in fulfilling His promises to His people. Therefore, it concerns God, as He loves His own glory, to be faithful in fulfilling His promises, and God looks at it as His glory to do it. Your comforts are dear to you and your preservation is dear to you, but God's glory is dearer to Him. Yea, God's glory is dearer to Him than your soul or your eternal state can be to you. The top of God's glory is His holiness, and His holiness consists in this, for one thing, His faithfulness to His promises.

Now for the application of this. From this you may observe whether or not you have ever understood God correctly. Let me put this question to you: what is that excellency of God that your soul closes with? We speak much of God's excellency and we all say that we love God, delight in God, and bless God. But now what is it in God that draws your heart to Him and causes your soul to love your God, to bless your God, and to delight in your God? What? Is it that God will show mercy to you, pardon your sin, save your soul and bring you to heaven? These are things that we ought to love and bless God for, but there must be more. It is the very person of God Himself that our hearts must be taken with, and it must be the person of God in His excellency, and what is that? His holiness!

Has the luster of the infinite holiness of God ever shone upon your heart and drawn your heart to Him? And has your heart ever leaped at the sight of the brightness of His holiness? Is this why you love Him? If so, you know God correctly and your heart has been correctly drawn to Him. David says, Psalm 119:140, *Thy word is very pure, therefore Thy servant loves it.* Can you say this? "O Lord, You are pure, You are holy, and therefore Your servant loves You. Your Word is holy and Your worship is holy, and Your servants are holy, and Your ordinances are holy, and therefore Your servants love all these." If the beauty of God's holiness is that which draws your heart forth in love to God, then proportionably it will be the beauty of holiness in all holy things that will draw your heart to love and delight in them. Then you will look upon His saints as glorious in holiness, upon His worship and Word and ordinances as glorious in holiness, and so your heart will be drawn to them. In Psalm 33:21, you see how the saints of God rejoiced in the Lord and had their hearts drawn to Him because of His holiness, *...for our hearts shall rejoice in Him because we have trusted in His holy name.* Trusting in God's holy name is that which makes our hearts rejoice in Him.

Secondly, from this the people of God should greatly comfort themselves in God in that they have to deal with Him as a holy God. Though they meet with much unholiness in the spirit of men with whom they converse, there is nothing in God but holiness, yea, the very beauty and glory of holiness. Brethren, it is a delightful thing, yea, a rare and blessed thing, to meet with a friend who has a clean and a pure heart, who has no mixture in him, who is holy in his ends and in his aims, who has a spirit free from guile. What rejoicing there is when one friend who has a pure and clean heart, free from guile, can meet with another such as himself and can close together in every point! But what a delight is it, then, to meet with a God who is infinite in purity and holiness, in whom there is no mixture at all! God takes delight in us because we have just some drops of His holiness. Oh, how should we rejoice in Him, then, who is infinite in holiness?

When we deal with men, we do not always find them to be what we expected. Many times we meet with men of excellent parts and gifts, but when we become intimate with them we do not find their ways and spirits suitable to the eminency and excellency of those parts and gifts. This is a grievous vexation to the saints, when they look upon men who are eminent and excellent and hope to find a proportion of spirit suitable thereunto, but instead they find an abundance of filth in their spirits. Though this may trouble you, bless your God in this that when you are to deal with God, you shall find nothing but holiness in Him. You shall find Him working according to His excellency, for I told you that was the nature of God's holiness. It is the perfection of His will whereby He works all things suitable to His eminency and excellency. Man has an excellency in him, but not always grace in his heart to work it suitably. But God always works suitable to His eminency and excellency. Now when our hearts are raised with the sight of God's excellency and we think that we shall always find God working according to it, what a comfort this is to a gracious soul against all the evil he meets with in the spirits of men among whom he converses.

For the further comfort of the saints, if God is glorious in holiness, so the saints are glorious in holiness, too. Remember the former point: as there is none like God, so there are none like His people; as a man's god is, so is he. That which can make an infinite God glorious must make a poor worm a glorious creature. It is true, that which will make a poor man glorious will not make a king glorious, but that which will make a king glorious must make a beggar glorious. Now holiness puts a luster and glory upon the divine nature itself, upon the infinite God, so that if you have it, it must put a glory upon you.

Therefore, it is observable that the communication of God's holiness to us is expressed in a different way than He communicates any other attribute to us. When God communicates His knowledge to us we are not said to partake of the divine nature by it, His power and the like. But when He communicates His holiness to us, we are then said to be made partakers of the divine nature. The holiness of the saints is the same as God's holiness, as it were, a beam of His. So the Scripture says in Heb. 12:10, *He chasteneth us for our profit, that we might be partakers of His holiness.* Mark it, "His holiness." Therefore it puts a wonderful glory and excellency on us, for it enables us to work as God and to live as God, for what is God's holiness, as I said before, but that by which He works to Himself as His final end, suitable to His own excellency?

So the saints come to work to God according to their measure as their final end, suitable to the infinite excellency of God Himself. They live as God lives and work as God works, and so are fitted to have communion with God. The life of a plant makes it unfit to have communion with beasts, nor the life of beasts with men, nor men with the life of God. Now holiness is the highest life of all beings, being the life of God. Therefore, it makes one fit for communion with God, for in communion there must be the same life.

Therefore, no creature can have communion with God who does not live the same life that God does, but if you partake of holiness, you live the life that God does and so are fit to have communion with God Himself.

Further, it puts not only a glory upon your person, but upon all you have and do. It sanctifies all. As the gold was sanctified by the altar, so the very natural actions and ways of God's common providence are sanctified to God's people. There is a luster upon all the good they enjoy by virtue of that holiness which God puts into them. As God's holiness puts a luster upon all His attributes, so holiness in the saints puts a luster into their parts, names, estates, and conversation with others. There is a beauty upon all by holiness. If a man of excellent parts has no holiness, there is no luster and beauty in him; but take a man who has able parts and holiness as well, oh, the luster that then appears in him!

Holiness is the very principle of eternal life, the very beginning of eternal life in the heart, and that which will certainly grow up to eternal life. Holiness is the proper object of God's delight. God does not delight in the legs of a man but in his holiness. Let a man be what he will, if God sees any impression of holiness in him, His soul closes with that soul.

Holiness is that which separates the creature for God and eternal life. There is a two-fold separation of a creature for God. You have the expression in Psalm 4:3, *The Lord hath set apart him that is godly for Himself.* He is set apart passively, and then he has an active principle to set apart himself for God. God, in His eternal election, sets apart those He intends to save for Himself. "Here are those," God says, "that I have set apart from the common lump of mankind to magnify the riches of My grace upon and to live with Me for all of eternity."

If God were to look from heaven upon a man or woman in the congregation and say, "Be it known to all the world that I, from eternity, have set apart such a man and woman to glorify them with Myself forever," everyone would look upon such a man or woman as glorious creatures indeed. But now know that if God has stamped the image of His holiness upon you, you have as much honor from God as if He had spoken thusly to you, and, in some respects, more. For if God were to declare that from all eternity you had been set apart from the creature for God, this would be glorious; but when God has put a principle of His own Spirit into you to enable you to get yourself apart and to consecrate yourself and all you have to God, this is more. In the other you are passive, but in this you are active.

There is more evil in unholiness than in reprobation. Men are afraid of reprobation, that God should set them apart from eternity to magnify the glory of His justice upon them, and this is truly terrible. But while you apprehend this as terrible, you are active in that which is more terrible. By the filthiness and wickedness of your heart and life you actively set yourself apart for eternal wrath and misery. The other is passive and you are only set apart, but in the wickedness of your heart you are active and set yourself apart. Holiness is the dedication of the creature to God, the separation of it from all other things to God by an active principle. On the other hand, sin is the separation of the creature by an active principle from God to all misery.

As holiness makes the name of God to be revered,

so holiness in the saints puts a reverend respect upon them in the very consciences of wicked men. Take the vilest of wicked men. Though they cry against you, if you walk strictly, your close walking with God will gain respect and reverence from their hearts in spite of their hearts. The reason why the people of God do not gain respect and esteem is because they do not walk strictly. Many men deceive themselves. They think that strictness is slighted and condemned and, therefore, they begin to lessen and abate in their exact walking. But this makes them unesteemed, and it is just with God that it should be so.

Does the abatement of holiness help you to gain more respect? No, walk more closely with God and you will have respect from men's consciences. Do what they can, you will anger their lust, but you will convince their consciences. In their most serious mood they will say, "Oh, that my soul were in this man's soul!" How often do they say so on their death beds! Holiness puts an excellency and glory on low and mean things. In the Law, what a glory it put on a piece of wood, or leather, or brass when it was consecrated to a holy use. That was God's ordinance. God put it in, not man. For a man to think that it is in the power of his will to make God esteem a creature, or that others in reference to God should esteem a creature more than what God has put into it is a great mistake. That I should put a divine excellency upon that which only has a natural excellency in it would be great boldness on my part, but if God's ordinance be so, then there is a glory put upon it, as in the temple. Because it was dedicated to God by divine institution, the very wood, brass, and everything had an excellency upon it. If ceremonial holiness puts such an excellency upon a piece of leather, then what shall the image of God put upon the immortal soul!

A further use is this: if God is glorious in holiness, then certainly God will maintain holiness in the world. This is one reason, among others, why this title is given to God, because He worked for His church. God will honor His own ordinances and worship, and will maintain His saints that are holy. "Preserve me, O Lord," said David, "for I am holy, and Thou wilt not give Thy holy one to see corruption." If you are God's holy one, He will not leave you to the power of corruption. He will defend you and maintain you. Therefore, says the Psalmist in Psalm 68:35, *O God, Thou art terrible out of Thy holy places.*

Are there any who will be injurious to God's people when they are in the way of His holy worship? God will be terrible out of His holy places unto such. These expressions are against the enemies of God, because it is the holiness of God and the people of God's holiness that they set themselves against. Let all men take heed what they do in opposing the saints and the ways of God's holy worship, for God will maintain holiness. Therefore, it concerns us all to honor holiness ourselves and to set up the glory of God's holiness as much as we can in the world. Let us all labor to be holy as our heavenly Father is holy. Let

Psalm 90:17 be our prayer, *Let the beauty of the Lord our God be upon us.* Oh, grow up more in holiness, which is the beauty of God. Converse much with God that you may be holy. When Moses was forty days in the mountain conversing with God, he came down with his face shining, and certainly those people who converse much with God will have their faces shine with holiness. There is much to be had by conversing with God who is a holy God.

Show forth the beauty of holiness in your conduct that others may say that if one beam of holiness is so delightful in a person, then how glorious in holiness is God Himself! I remember what a heathen said of the God of the Christians when he saw their courage. He said that the God of the Christians is a great God. Let us walk so holily before others that they can read holiness in our conduct and be forced to say that the God of this people is a holy God. Especially look to your heart, to cleanse it when you draw near to this holy God in this holy worship. Then labor to sanctify His name. Look to your feet. Do not come in your filth into the presence of so holy a God.

It is a notable expression of Joshua in Joshua 24:19, when the people say, *We will serve the Lord, for He is our God.* Joshua said, *You cannot serve the Lord, for He is a holy God.* It is as if he should say, "It is another manner of business to serve the Lord than you think, for you have to deal with a holy God. External worship will not serve His turn."

It is proof that people do not know God when they

can turn His service off so slightly. The sight of God would put you in another frame. If you knew God in His holiness, you would look upon the service of God as a great service. You would serve a holy God. As I Samuel 6:20 says, *Who can stand before this holy God?* If you apprehended God to be a holy God, your heart would be stricken with fear and awe, and you would say, "Who can stand before this holy God?" Psalm 89:7 says, *God is greatly to be feared in the assembly of His saints, and to be had in reverence of those that are round about Him.* God is to be held in reverence by all men, but if you come near Him, then you must labor to sanctify your hearts. How can you come before the luster and beauty of God's holiness with willfull uncleanness in your heart? Job 13:11 is a remarkable text, *Shall not His excellency make you afraid?* You have heard that God's holiness is His excellency, so I say to you that have to deal with Him, shall not His excellency make you afraid? Are you conscious of your uncleanness, and do you come into the presence of a holy God and not fear and tremble before Him? O what a bold, daring heart you have that can come into the presence of a holy God with an unholy heart and not tremble. It would be of admirable use in all our dealings with God to have clear apprehensions of His holiness.

Labor to magnify God this way. As God is glorious in holiness, so set Him out in His glory by keeping His worship pure. It is a special thing God looks at, that we take heed of what we do in defiling His worship. God's ordinances are the beauty of His holiness. Therefore we must labor to come pure and clean to them. It is that which God commands His church, to keep the vessels of His sanctuary holy, and those are the ordinances. In Exodus 20:24-25, God gives them charge to make Him an altar, but God says, *If thou wilt make Me an altar of stone, thou shalt not build it of hewn stone: for if thou lift up thy tool upon it, thou hast polluted it.*

"What," they might say, "shall we have an altar of rude stone? Shall we not polish it and make it fine and sumptuous? Will not that make it more attractive to look at?"

"No," says God, "if you lift up a tool on it you pollute it." We are apt to think that such and such mixtures of men and such and such ceremonies would make the worship of God glorious, but this is a great mistake.

It is a normal thing for whores to paint their faces. They will not be content with their natural beauty but are more pompous in their apparel than the chaste matrons are. It is so with the whore of Babylon. How glorious are they in all their worship? What strange things do they have to take the outwards senses, not having the purity of God's worship? Certainly these things defile the worship of God. Compare two texts for this. Isaiah 44:9, *They that make a graven image are all of them vanity, and their delectable things shall not profit.* Mark it, the images of idolaters are delectable things in their esteem, but see what God says of them, Ezek.7:20, *As for the beauty of His ornament, He set it in majesty, but they made them images of their abominations, and of their detestable things therein.* They call them delectable things, but God calls them detestable. But when God speaks of His own ordinances, He says that He set the beauty of His ornament in majesty.

Oh, the worship of God in the plainness and simplicity of the gospel! It is the ornament of God, the beauty of His ornament, and the beauty of His ornament set in majesty! What phrases are here? This is God's worship, but if man mixes anything of his own in God's worship it is detestable to God. Therefore, if we would honor and magnify God in His holiness, let us keep His worship pure, for holiness becomes the worship of God forever.

The consideration of this should humble us and make us ashamed for the remainder of the unholiness that is in our hearts. The sight of God's holiness made Isaiah cry out, Isaiah 6:5, *Woe is me for I am undone, because I am a man of unclean lips, and I dwell in the midst of a people of unclean lips, for mine eyes have seen the King, the Lord of hosts.* Certainly there is nothing in the world that has the power to humble the heart as much as God's holiness. Your heart is correctly humbled for sin when you look on it as that which is opposed to the pure nature of God. I am not only troubled for my sin because I am afraid it will bring hell along with it, but because I have had a sight of the infinite holiness of God and the purity of His nature. I have a nature so filthy and opposite to that infinite holiness of His. Hereby examine your hearts whether your humiliation is right or not. It is a good argument when the infinite holiness of God has made you see your uncleanness and, upon that, has humbled you.

Lastly, what need we all have of Jesus Christ. If God is glorious in holiness, we should all say, "Who can stand before so holy a God!" Were it not for the holiness of the blessed Mediator who stands between the Father and us, and presents His infinite satisfaction to the Father for our sins, and clothes us with His righteousness, woe, woe unto us! If you could possibly imagine that all of the excellencies of heaven and earth were put into one creature except holiness, if that creature had only the least drop of uncleanness and unholiness in it, God would eternally hate that creature. Were there not a Mediator between that creature and God, God would eternally let out His wrath upon it, for God is so glorious in holiness that He infinitely hates filthiness. We wonder when we hear of the great misery threatened to wicked men, but we would not wonder if we knew God's holiness.

God so infinitely hates sin that he instantly sent all the angels that fell down in chains of eternal darkness and refused to enter into the least parley with them or to be reconciled with them. Now what is the reason that, though we have so much uncleanness in us, God is pleased to be reconciled to us, and admits us into His presence and gives us hope to see His face with joy to all eternity? It is this: because we have a Mediator and they have none. Were it not for that, we could weep streams of blood from our eyes and God would hate and abhor us. His wrath would eternally seize us.

Therefore, though you may rejoice in inherent holiness, let your hearts be particularly upon the perfect holiness of Jesus Christ and offer that up to God. Though you have much uncleanness in yourself and in your duties (for what is it for us to offer duty to the holy God), let this comfort you. You do not have to deal with God in yourself but through Christ, and in Him you have liberty to come. You may look upon God's face with boldness. This is the great mystery of godliness revealed in the gospel, that, notwithstanding the infiniteness of God's holiness, there is a way for us polluted creatures to look upon this God with joy. This mystery is only taught in the gospel. Though men now think they can come and cry to you, and you come to see your uncleanness, your heart will sink down in eternal despair. You will not be able to endure beholding God then. And if you are not acquainted with God in this way of reconciliation, you will be undone forever. Therefore, study the mystery of the gospel. Make use of Christ that the glory of God's holiness may not be to your terror but to your comfort.

It has not been long since, as some of you may remember, that the subject of the saints' enjoyment of God was handled in this place out of I Cor.15:28. At that time I told you that we had such an expression in Scripture only twice, applied to God in the happiness of the saints' enjoyment of Him in heaven and applied here to Christ, of what Christ is to them for the present. That which was handled about God's being all in all is the end. This which is to be delivered concerning Christ being all in all is that which brings the soul to the blessed end. As Christ Himself says, John 14:1, *Ye believe in God, believe also in Me.* So I say, as God shall be all in all eternally to the saints, if you believe in that, believe also in this which I am to deliver to you this day, that Christ is all and in all.

The Apostle Paul was a chosen vessel to bear the name of Christ, to carry it up and down in the world. Indeed, his spirit was full of Christ. He desired to know nothing but Christ, to preach nothing but Christ, to be found in none but Christ. The very name of Christ was delightful to him. He seeks to magnify Christ in all of his epistles and, in these words I read to you, he omnifies Christ. He does not only make Him great, but he makes Him all. *There is neither Greek nor Jew, circumcision nor uncircumcision, barbarian, Scythian, bond nor free, but Christ is all and in all.* That is, there is no privilege in the one to commend them to God, and there is no lack of anything in the other to hinder them from God. Let men be what they will in their outward respects, what is that to God? Let them be never so mean in regard of all outward things, that can never hinder them from the enjoyment of God, for God does not look at these things, but Christ is all and in all to them.

As far as God sees Christ in anyone, He accepts them. If Christ is not there, no matter what they have, He does not regard them. Christ is all in all, even in the esteem of the Father Himself. He was the delight of the Father from all eternity, Prov.8:30, and the Father undertook infinite contentment in Him upon His willingness to undertake this blessed work of the redemption of mankind. God the Father is infinitely satisfied in Christ. He is all in all to Him. Surely if Christ is an object sufficient for the satisfaction of the Father, much more, then, is He an object sufficient for the satisfaction of any soul.

But that which is the main scope of the Holy Ghost here is this high expression of Christ's transcendent excellency, which I will deliver in this doctrinal proposition: Christ is the only means of conveyance of good that God the Father intends to communicate unto the children of men in order to eternal life; He is all in all. This which I am to preach to you now, namely God's communicating Himself in His mercy to mankind through a Mediator, is the very sum of the gospel, the great mystery of godliness. It is the chief part of the mind and counsel of God that He would have made known to the children of men in this world. This is the great message that the ministers of the gospel have to bring to the sons and daughters of men, and it is the most absolutely necessary point in all theology.

That which I shall this day endeavor is to show you something of the glory of God shining in this truth: that God communicates Himself through a Mediator, through His Son. This is the great point of theology that is absolutely necessary for you to know if you would have eternal life. It is possible to be ignorant of many other truths and still be saved, but there must be something of this or there can be no salvation. The mistake in this very thing is the miscarriage and the eternal undoing of thousands upon thousands of souls. Many believe that they have need of, and can never be saved without, God's mercy. The light of nature convinces us of this. But they are ignorant of, and do not see the reality of, this truth: that God communicates His mercy through a Mediator. They miscarry and perish eternally with cries to God for mercy because they come to God, but not through a Mediator.

This is the sum of the gospel and the most supernatural truth revealed in all the Book of God. It is a truth that was hidden from nearly all the world for many ages. The Scripture says, I Cor.2:8, *The princes of the world knew it not.* It is a truth of which we are unable to understand anything by the light of nature, I Cor.1:21, *The world by wisdom knew not God.* That is, by all their arts and sciences, by all their natural wisdom, they did not know God savingly. They did not know God in Christ. There are no footsteps of this truth in all the works of creation or providence. Therefore in Eph.3:8, Paul says that he was appointed to preach *the unsearchable riches of Christ,* the riches that have no footsteps (that is the proper meaning of the words). There are no footsteps of the riches of the gospel in the creature. Therefore you cannot trace it there, whereas many other points of religion have many footsteps in the creature. By the light of nature much may be discovered about God, as that all our good consists in communion with God, that when we have offended God we must seek for pardon and mercy from Him, and so on. But that God communicates Himself through Christ, and that not one drop of mercy that leads to eternal life can be communicated from God except through Christ the Mediator, there is not one footstep of this in all the works of God.

This is that which is so supernatural, that is above perfect nature. Adam knew nothing of this in his perfect state. This is that into which the angels themselves desire to pry, looking on it as a mighty depth. I Peter 1:12 says that the angels stoop down, for so the word signifies. It is as if something is lying in a deep pit, and when the angels see it they stoop down with their bodies to pry into the pit. That's the proper meaning of the word. So the angels see a mighty depth in the mystery of the gospel and they stoop down to pry into it that they may know what it is. This is that which requires a work of the Spirit, beyond the ordinary work of the Spirit of God, to reveal it to the soul. Paul the Apostle, speaking in I Cor.2:10 of the mystery of the gospel, says, *The spirit that searcheth the deep things of God* reveals this; that is, the Spirit of God in His extraordinary work. As He is a Spirit searching the deep things of God, so He is a revealing Spirit of this truth unto us and, therefore, seeing it so, it is not to be passed over lightly.

"Aye," you will say, "it is true. All must come through Jesus Christ." Well, you see a little at first, but there is much more in this truth than we are aware of. This is a truth that is the most profitable of all the truths contained in the Book of God. There is no growing up in godliness until we come to know God in Christ. The knowledge of God is something to work upon the heart and may labor against their sin because they see it as against the Law of God. They set upon duties because God requires it of them, and this is good, but until they come to understand the mystery of the gospel, of God's letting Himself out unto His people through a Mediator, they only bungle in the ways of godliness. They do not thrive and grow up in them, and therefore those Christians who live under a ministry where many good truths are revealed to them, but they only have a little of the mystery of Christ as the Mediator, do not sanctify God in their conduct. Their way of Christianity is low.

I remember a speech that Erasmus had when they wanted him to write something against Luther, and promised him a bishopric if he would do it. He said, "Luther is greater than that I can write against him; for

I am instructed more in one small page of Luther than out of whole Thomas Aquinas." That was the great schoolman. So certainly understanding only one small truth, one sentence in the mystery of the gospel in a way of God's communicating Himself unto us through Jesus Christ, instructs the soul and causes it to thrive and grow up in godliness abundantly more than thousands of sermons about mere morality.

You have an admirable text for this in Eph.3:17 and so on, *That Christ may dwell in your hearts by faith, that ye being rooted and grounded in love, may be able to comprehend with all saints, what is the breadth, and length, and depth, and height, and to know the love of Christ, which passeth knowledge.* Mark what follows, *that ye might be filled with the fulness of God,* v.19. By coming to know God in Christ, that is, to know Christ to be God's way of communicating Himself to us, we come to be filled with all the fulness of God. The hearts of many Christians are very scant and empty. There is not a fulness in their spirits, and all because they know so little of God in Christ in this mystery of the gospel.

Lastly, there is no truth revealed in all the Scriptures whereby we can honor God as much as this. This, indeed, is the great honor that God would have in the world, to be honored in His Son and in the great design He has of bringing forth glorious things by His Son and, therefore, though we know never so much of God and would honor Him merely as the Creator of heaven and earth, yet God does not accept that honor. That is only to honor Him in a natural way. We never know what it is to honor God correctly so as to be accepted by Him until we come to honor Him in an evangelical way, to honor Him in His Son. Yet the greatest honor He has from most in this world, even from multitudes in the very church of God who hear the mystery of Christ opened to them, is offered to Him merely in a natural way and not in this spiritual, evangelical service of God. You see the consequence of the point, now let us fall to it.

First, I shall show you the truth of it in Scripture.

Secondly, how it comes to pass that there can be no good communicated to us from God leading to eternal life but by Christ.

Thirdly, how Christ comes to be the means and way of conveying all good to us from His Father.

Fourthly, I shall mention some special things, great things, wherein most of the goodness of God is communicated to us, and show you how Christ is all in all to us in them.

And fifthly, the reasons why God uses this way of communicating Himself to us through His Son; why He does not communicate Himself immediately to us but through a Mediator. These are the five things for the doctrinal part.

For the first, the course of Scripture runs this way, especially the New Testament. You know that Christ said, John 14:6, *I am the way, the truth and the life; no man cometh unto the Father but by Me*. There is no coming to the Father but by Christ. He is the way. The

Apostle says in I Cor.3, *All things are yours, whether Paul, or Apollo, or Cephas, or the world, or life, or death, or things present, or things to come, all are yours.* How is that? Mark it, *All are yours, and ye are Christ's, and Christ is God's.* God the Father is the principle of all good. All comes from Him first, but it does not come from Him immediately. He does not say all are yours for you are God's, because you have an interest in God, all therefore comes to be yours. No, but *all is yours and you are Christ's, and Christ is God's.* So you see here how Christ comes between you and God.

All good is in God, true, but how shall we come to partake of that good? There is such a distance between you and God that, were not Christ in the middle, you would never come together. But Christ has come between and joined you together so that all is yours because you are Christ's and Christ is God's. Think of God as the Fountain of all good, and Christ, as it were, the Cistern, and from Him are pipes converged to every believer. Faith sucks at the mouth of every pipe and draws from God, but it comes from God through Christ. The Father fills the Son with all good and so it comes from the Father, through the Son, by faith unto the soul of every believer. We have a notable expression of this mystery in Ephesians, the second and third chapters. In chapter 2:12, Paul has told them that they had been without hope and without God in the world, but, he says in verse 13, *Ye who were sometimes far off are made nigh by the blood of Christ.* It is by the blood of Christ that you have anything to do with God. But especially in Eph.3:12, *In whom we have boldness and access with confidence by the faith of Him.* In whom? In Christ we come to have boldness and access. The word "boldness" signifies liberty of speech. We can come before God with liberty of speech, and we also have access. We are led by the hand of Christ to the Father. There is no coming to the Father except by Christ, and Christ takes a believer by the hand and leads him to the Father, and so he comes to have boldness.

Suppose that a traitor were to be banished by the court, and later the Prince desires to be the means of reconciliation with the King. He would come and take the traitor by the hand and say to him, "Come, I will lead you in my hand to my father, and, though you have provoked him, being in my hand you need not be afraid. You may go to him with boldness and confidence." In Christ we have boldness and access with confidence, and although before there was a dreadful breach between us and the Father, now being led by by the hand of Christ there is access and freedom of speech for us. The truth is clear enough in the whole tenor of the gospel.

How can it be that, though God is in Himself the Fountain of all goodness and infinite mercy, there is still a stoppage, as it were, so that not one drop of His mercy can be communicated to the children of men except in this way? Although we have to deal with God, who in His own nature is infinitely merciful, yet such is the case with man, such are the terms between God and man, that not one drop of this infinite ocean can ever be expected to come from God except by this way.

This is how it comes to pass: first, because of the breach of the first covenant that God made with mankind. Only men and angels, the human and angelic nature, are capable of a covenant with God, if we speak of a covenant properly, and because they are capable of this way of God's proceeding with them, God goes according to the nature of His creature. Therefore, He first makes a covenant with them, intending to convey and communicate His goodness to them by that covenant. This covenant now being broken, and a breach existing between God and man, there is a stoppage made by virtue of that breach. There is now no good to be had by virtue of the first covenant and, unless there is a second, there can be no good expected at all. The first is broken and we are lost because of that.

Further, there is such an infinite distance between God and us that there can be no coming together. That is not so much due to God's excellency in Himself and our lowliness that we are such poor, low creatures as it is due to the infiniteness of His holiness and our uncleanness and sinfulness. This makes the distance.

Besides this, there is the strength of the law. The curse of the law is upon every soul naturally and this stops His mercy. There was never a vessel sealed more tightly to keep from having a drop of liquor poured into it than the curse of the law puts a seal upon every soul to keep mercy from it, as far as God looks upon it merely in its natural state and not through His Son.

Then there are the cries of infinite justice against men, which must have satisfaction, and until justice is satisfied, mercy does not stir unless it is in a way of providing satisfaction unto justice. Put these two together, the breach of the first covenant, the distance between God and man because of God's holiness and man's sinfulness, and the power of the curse of the law upon man and the cries of divine justice that will never be quiet until it has received satisfaction. If these things are rightly apprehended, we will see how far off from receiving mercy from God we are, even though He is an infinite Fountain of mercy, unless there is some strange way of conveying it to us.

We know from God's dealing with the fallen angels that there is no way of conveying mercy to them. They are left to perish forever. The thousands of angels that fell from God have been thousands of years crying out for mercy and cannot obtain one drop. Why? Because there is no Mediator between God and them, and it would have been our case too, had there not been a Mediator between God and us. Many think that if they are sensible of their sins and can believe that God is infinitely merciful, they shall do well enough. But I must tell you that though there is infinite mercy in God, if you have no interest in Christ you will be undone forever!

But how is Christ all in all to us in God's communication of good to us?

The first ground of all is the covenant that God the Father made with His Son from all eternity past. Therefore in Titus 1:2, the Apostle speaks of the promise that was before the world began. Now this promise can only mean that covenant which passed between the Father and the Son, and therefore, the Apostle says in I Cor.2:9-10, *Eye hath not seen, nor ear heard, neither have entered into the heart of man, the things which God hath prepared for them which love Him: but the Spirit which searcheth all things, yea the deep things of God, He hath revealed unto us;* that is, the Spirit of God in the gospel reveals what were the eternal thoughts and purposes of God concerning us and what the transactions were between the Father and the Son in reference to mankind before the world was. The covenant being between the Father and the Son, and the Father requiring in this covenant satisfaction to infinite divine justice, Christ yields to this.

Therefore, in the second place, Christ actually comes to be the way of conveyance by taking our nature upon Himself and so making us reconcilable to God by taking human nature into such a close union to the divine nature, to the second person in the Trinity. There are two great mysteries in the gospel: one, that there should be divers persons in one nature (this is the mystery of the Trinity), and the other that there should be divers natures in one person (this is the mystery of the hypostatic union of our nature with Christ). So that Christ, taking man's nature into such a close union to Himself was a mighty preparative for God to have thoughts of peace toward human nature rather than angels. It was one part of His humility and therefore has a meritorious efficiency in this work of reconciling God to man, but this was not sufficient.

Therefore, in the third place, Christ was content to come into the world and be made the head of a second covenant between God and mankind, to perform whatever the Father should require for the satisfaction of divine justice. As Adam, by being the head of the first covenant, was the means of conveying all evil to us, so Christ, by being the head of the second covenant, is the means of conveying all good to us. By His subjecting to this, we come to receive all grace and mercy from God. It could not have been otherwise, for though God would have thought of a second covenant, had He left it to us to perform the terms of it, we would have broken that one as soon as we did the first. But because Christ undertook to be the head of the second covenant and performed whatever the Father required in it by His perfect obedience to the Law and satisfaction to divine justice, divine justice had nothing to lay to the charge of those for whom Christ undertook satisfaction.

This was a mighty way of letting out God's grace and mercy to the souls of believers, for what is it that stops the current of His mercy? It is the curse of the Law and cries of divine justice. But now, Christ undertaking to undergo that curse and satisfy divine justice, God has as much honor now by His suffering as He had dishonor by man's sinning. Man's sin is made up in this, and it is what justice requires. "I have had dishonor by sin," says justice, "I must have this dishonor made up by suffering, and so much suffering that in it I will have as much honor as I had dishonor in sinning." These are the conditions upon which God will be reconciled to man, and upon no other.

I beg you to consider this, and herein you will see the infinite necessity of Christ. God is with us upon these terms. God says, "You have sinned against Me and dishonored Me. How do you think to be delivered?"

Why, Lord, You are merciful!

"Aye," says God, "but I am resolved upon this: I will have as much honor by suffering as I had dishonor by sinning."

Lord, what would have become of us if we had been left to make up this breach!

This is the very reason why the damned in hell are there eternally, because they are there upon these terms. God says, "I am infinite and I am dishonored, and there they must lie until I have as much honor by their suffering as I had dishonor by their sinning." Now after they have been there thousands of thousands of years, the honor of God calls for still more, and therefore they must lie there forever. But now Christ, who is the great Saviour, comes and enters into covenant with God, and, fulfilling that covenant, He lays down such a price to God that God shall have as much honor by His suffering for sin as He had dishonor before in the committing of sin. This being done, the current of mercy is unstopped, the passages of it are opened, and God, being infinite in grace and mercy in Himself, makes a glorious way for the streams of His mercy to issue and flow forth to the children of men.

In this way we may see that God, in forgiving sin and showing mercy to sinful creatures, is just and goes in a way of justice as well as a way of mercy. Therefore that text in Romans 3:25-26 is very observable (a text whose meaning troubled Luther considerably for awhile), *Whom God hath set forth to be a propitiation, through faith in His blood, to declare His righteousness for the remission of sins that are past, through the forbearance of God. To declare, I say, at this time His righteousness, that He might be just, and the justifier of him which believeth in Jesus.* What troubled Luther so much was that God should declare His righteousness in the remission of sins. Everyone knows that God declares His mercy, but that God declares His righteousness, and that Christ is sent to be a propitiation so that God might declare His righteousness, may seem strange. The Holy Ghost repeats the phrase, "to declare His righteousness," as if He should say, "Consider that God, in the pardoning of sin, not only manifests His grace and mercy, but declares His righteousness that he might be just and the justifier of one who believes in Jesus." Not merciful, but just. Thus we see the way Christ takes to be the means of conveying God's goodness to us: by performing the covenant and so satisfying divine justice.

Lastly, He is the way of conveying good to us, as

by His satisfaction, so by His intercession, for He is now and shall forever be at the right hand of the Father in glory making intercession for His people. That is, He is continually presenting before the Father the work of His mediation, His merits, what He has done and suffered and is, as it were, pleading with His Father for the conveyance of all needful mercy and good unto the souls and bodies of His people whom He has redeemed. It is as if He should every moment eternally speak thus to the Father: "Father, behold, here is My blood, My merits, My death, all My sufferings, the work of My humiliation. It is for these, yea, for this poor soul and for that poor soul particularly." Know that Christ thinks not only of the lump of believers in general, but particularly of every believer, and is continually presenting His infinite merits before the Father to plead with Him for the supplying of all grace and mercy to us. Thus, He becomes an infinite way of conveying good to the souls of His people, and to be all and in all to them both here and eternally.

But now the fourth, and that is to give examples of some special things we have from God and to manifest that Christ is all in all in those things. In the point of justification and the pardon of sins, the great thing we stand in need of from God is the acceptation of us as righteous. Christ is all in all to us here, that is the tenor of the gospel, Rom.3:24, *being justified freely by His grace, through the redemption that is in Jesus Christ.* Luther had this expression concerning justification: "In the point of justification, there Christ and faith must only be put together; they must be alone, and nothing else with them. But in our conduct, there is where good works come in, just as it is between the bridegroom and the bride. The bridegroom and the bride are alone in the bridal chamber, but when they travel, they have their train and servants attending them." So he compares justification to the bridal chamber, none but Christ and faith must be there, but when they go abroad in their conduct, then all other graces attend them and good works come in, but Christ is all in all here.

Our justification is not made up by what we have done or all that we can possibly do. You will say, "True, we have done little." But suppose any of you should do your utmost in any particular that God requires. You will say, "I hope if I can do what I can that God will accept it." No, you made a great mistake if you think this. People are very apt to look upon God as if the terms between God and them were no other than this: God is full of pity and mercy and we are weak and can only do a little, but if we do what we are able, God will accept the will for the deed. No, God does not accept the will for the deed in the point of justification. It is true in those that are already justified that God accepts the will for the deed in the performance of a duty, so as to take delight in them, but in the point of justification, pardoning sin and acceptance to righteousness, He must there have perfect obedience. Though we endeavor never so much, unless we can bring to God a perfect righteousness, we are undone forever. Woe to Abraham, woe to Isaac, woe to Jacob, woe to David and Daniel and all the prophets and apostles, notwithstanding all their righteousness, if they did not have a righteousness beyond what was in themselves. If they had not had a perfect righteousness to offer to their Father, they would have been utterly lost forever.

Therefore, it is not for you to rest upon the fact that you do what you can, have good wishes and desires and the like, for if all the righteousness of all the righteous men who ever lived were in one man, it would not be sufficient for his justification. It is not what God enables you to do either, that can be the formality of your justification. Such are the terms between God and you that there is nothing you can do of yourself, or be enabled to do, that is accepted by Him for your righteousness to eternal life.

But it may be said, "It is true that, even though God might enable me, there will be imperfections; but God is merciful and will pass them by." Therefore I add another consideration. It is not only what you can do or be enabled to do, but it is not the addition of God's mercy that can eke out your justification. (I am speaking of the mercy of God as a Creator to His creature and not under the consideration through Christ, and accepting a righteousness beyond your own.) This is a great mistake. Many think that what they have in themselves and what they are able to do is only a little, but when they have done something, if God will come and add His mercy, they think it will eke it out. No, it is not that and mercy together that is your justification.

To understand it more clearly, think of it this way: the work of God's mercy in justification is not to be used to be our justification, nor will it eke out what we are lacking. The work of God's mercy in justifying a soul is to take him off of himself, to unbottom him, and to make him see and be sensible of his own unrighteousness and uncleanness. This is a great and mighty work of God's mercy.

I remember that Luther said of himself that, while he was a papist, he was not obedient out of worldly respects for a livelihood and the like. He did what he did out of conscience, and yet he says afterward (after he knew God in Christ), "That which I counted gain was loss to me." He did not think it enough to do what he did out of conscience and that God's mercy would make up the rest. No, he was taken off of that way. It is not the work of mercy to do this, but to reveal to the soul a righteousness of a higher nature, of the Mediator between God and man, and to enable the soul by faith to offer up that righteousness to God the Father for satisfaction. This is the work of God's mercy in the point of justification. The mistake of the way of God's mercy having an influence unto our justification is a very dangerous mistake. We need to be very wary in this great point of justification, for all depends on it. I remember Luther said that it was an easy matter to say we close with God's grace and the righteousness of Christ alone in the point of justification until the soul is brought into a conflict. Then it is the hardest thing in the world to do, and the people of God have found it so in the time of trouble of conscience. Thus the first point, Christ is all in all in justification.

Secondly, He is all in all in point of adoption, Gal.3:26, *For ye are all the children of God by faith in Christ Jesus,* and chapter 4:4-5, *But when the fulness of time was come, God sent forth His Son made of a woman, made under the law, to redeem them that were under the law, that we might receive the adoption of sons.* And especially John 1:12, *But as many as received Him, to them He gave power to become the sons of God, even to them that believe on His name.* The word translated "power" is another word in the Greek. He gave them authority to become the sons of God. It is a word that imports more than the bare power. Everyone will challenge a part in sonship who is a child of God, but only those who are in Christ have authority to challenge it as their due.

If a stranger should say that he was the king's son and heir to the crown, it would cost him his life because he is not the king's son. But if one is declared by an act of Parliament to be the rightful heir to the crown, then he has authority to challenge it. It is so here. When once we come to be in Christ, then we have authority to claim this privilege, to be sons of God and heirs of heaven. This great privilege that is so mightily above us we have in Christ, not only by way of the redundancy of His merits, but by our union with Him. We are married to Christ and, by union with His person, are made one with Him. So we are sons by virtue of His sonship and are therefore sons of God in a higher way than are the angels. The angels are sons by creation, but we are the sons of God in Christ by virtue of our union in His sonship. As Christ is the Son of God, the second person in the Trinity and we are made one with Him, we come to be the sons of God in a mystical way of union with Him, and Christ is all in all in that.

In point of reconciliation and peace with God, Christ is all in all there, *being justified by faith, we have peace with God through our Lord Jesus Christ,* Rom.5:1. All the created power in heaven and earth cannot bring peace to a troubled soul. There is no salve for a wounded spirit but the blood of Christ applied to it. He is that brazen serpent that only is able to cure the strings of conscience. As Luther says, it is a harder matter to comfort an afflicted conscience than to raise the dead. Few think it so and wonder what people mean in being so troubled in conscience. I tell you, were there not a mighty Redeemer, the conscience of a man or woman could never be pacified once they apprehend the wrath of God against them. So Christ is all in all here.

And He is all in all in point of all our sanctification, that is sanctification to life. There is a general kind of sanctification the Scripture speaks of which comes some way from Christ, but now I speak of that sancti-fication which is our spiritual life. You know what the Scripture says, John 3:36, *He that believeth on the Son, hath everlasting life;* and John 1:16, *And of His fulness have we all received and grace for grace.* There is the fulness of Christ conveyed to the soul, so that our sanctification is not only from Him meritoriously, but efficiently and, in a way, materially, too. For He not only merits it and works by His Spirit, but through our union with Him there is a flowing of sanctification from Him into us as the principle of our life. From the liver there flows blood into all the parts of the body. So through our union with Christ, who has the fulness of the Godhead in Him, sanctification flows from Him like a fountain into the souls of the saints.

There sanctification does not come so much from their struggling endeavors, vows, and resolutions as it comes flowing to them from their closing with Christ and their union with Him. There may be a great deal of striving and endeavoring that may be utterly ineffectual for lack of having recourse unto Christ as the spring and wellhead of all grace and holiness. I remember a German divine who professed of himself that before he understood the grace of Christ in the gospel, he vowed and vowed, covenanted and covenanted a thousand times, and could never overcome his corruptions until he understood God's letting out His grace through Christ. Then he got strength against them.

The reason why we fail in point of sanctification is because we think we get it all by main strength, but the ready way is to close with Christ by faith and then there will flow in life and grace to the soul. There may be many moralities by the light of nature and the remainder of that light left in us, but that is not the sanctification that is to life. And, hence, it is that there is so much beauty and glory in the sanctification of the saints, because Christ is all in all in it. There is such power and strength in it because it is of the strength of Christ, for Christ is all in all in it. And, hence, it is of an abiding nature and an immortal seed and, therefore, of a higher nature than that of Adam in innocency. That was lost but not this, because Christ is all in all in it so that Christ is all in all in our sanctification likewise.

Again, He is all in all in the lack of things, whatever it is that we lack. Do we lack grace, do we lack gifts, do we lack outward comforts in the world? There is enough in Christ. It is Christ that is instead of all, that is better than all, and that will supply all in His due time. Those who know Christ and have acquaintance with Him, though they have this and that comfort taken from them, they still know how to make supply out of Christ. They have that skill and art and mystery of godliness that they can make Christ to be all in all in the lack of all, and it is a great skill and mystery of godliness to know how to make up all in Christ in the lack of all.

Again, to the saints, Christ is all in all in the enjoyment of all. When they enjoy never so much of the creature comforts, Christ is all in all to them. The satisfaction that their souls have is not that they have larger estates, more friends, or greater comforts than others, but that they know how to enjoy Christ in all, and can look upon it as a fruit of the covenant that God made with them in Christ and as coming down from the fountain of God's eternal love and mercy in His Son, Zech.9:11. God says there, *As for thee also, by the blood of thy covenant, I have sent forth thy prisoners out of the pit wherein there is no water*. That which is spoken there of the deliverance of the prisoners may be applied to all the mercies that a believer enjoys. Whatever deliverance he has from evil, whatever good he is possessed of, is by the blood of the covenants.

A believer can look upon every bit of meat he has, and upon all the good he enjoys, and can see it all come streaming to him in the blood of Christ. And so it comes more sweetly. The sun does not shine as warm through the air as it does through a magnifying glass. Take a magnifying glass and hold it between you and the sun and the glass will contract the beams of the sun so that it shall have an efficacy of heat, even to burn again. So the goodness of God that comes to people through the general bounty and patience of God does not have an efficacy to warm and heat their hearts, to draw them to God. But now Christ is, as it were, the magnifying glass that is held between God and the soul, and how the mercy that comes through this magnifying glass warms and heats outward comforts! Therefore, there are no people in the world who can enjoy outward comforts with as much fulness of contentment as do the people of God, because they all come to them through Christ. Christ is all in all in the enjoyment of all, and so I might show you how He will be all in all in heaven to eternity.

But to give you one more particular. As He is all in all in the good we have from God, so He is all in all in whatever we offer up to God: as in descent from God to us, so in ascent from us to God. Christ must come in here. He must be all in all in our services. Though our services be never so good, though they are spiritual, they must still find acceptance with the Father through Christ. That text in I Pet.2:5 is very remarkable for this, *Ye also, as lively stones, are built up a spiritual house, an holy priesthood, to offer up spiritual sacrifices acceptable to God by Jesus Christ.* Mark, to offer up spiritual sacrifices. But though the sacrifice is spiritual, that is not enough to make it acceptable. Christ must come in. Therefore he adds, *acceptable to God by Jesus Christ.*

Many people offer up sacrifices and they think that is enough. But the people of God do not rest in the duty alone, nor in the spirituality of the duty, though that is counted as a great matter. They go one step higher, and so must you in all the duties you offer up to God. That is, do not only be careful that your duties are spiritual, but you must offer them to God in the hands of Jesus Christ and expect acceptance through Him. When you deal with God in all your approaches to Him, be sure that you do not omit the work of faith in laying hold of Christ and carrying Him along with you or else your service will not be accepted.

Though the sacrifices in the law were never so good, they were not accepted unless a man brought them to the priest, who offered up the sacrifice, and then it was accepted. That was to signify to us the priestly office of Christ. This is the very work of the priestly office of Christ: to take all our sacrifices that we offer up to the Father and offer them up for us. We must not presume to offer them up ourselves. Though they offered a sacrifice that was never so good, if they did not offer it upon the right altar, it was not accepted. So Christ is the right Altar upon which we must offer up all our sacrifices to the Father. We must look towards the temple, towards Christ, in all that goes from us unto God, Christ being all in all for acceptation of our duties. Thus we have finished with the fourth particular, showing wherein Christ is all in all.

But now it may be demanded how it comes to pass that God will have this way of communicating Himself to mankind and will not go in another way that we, by the light of nature and reason, think He should go? True, indeed, we are sinners. Aye, but God is merciful and we will seek and cry to Him for pardon, mercy, and deliverance from our sins, and what need is there for more? Why will God not save us in this way? I will not stand now to dispute about the possibility of this, but we know this is not the way.

We are therefore now to inquire why God would rather take this strange way than go another way. Indeed, it is a wonderful way if we consider it rightly. There is nothing in the world that works so much upon a man's heart to adore and admire God in the mystery of the gospel as the understanding of this: that God should have a peculiar way of communicating Himself to man, different from the angels and all other creatures. It must be through the second person of the Trinity, and He must take man's nature upon Him and suffer and die, and all the mercy we have must be through Him. This is a wonderful mystery of godliness and should take up our serious thoughts in the consideration of it.

Now if you would know the reason for it, the first thing is this: that hereby God might manifest to all the children of men what a dreadful breach their sins have made between God and them. We cannot imagine any other way that this breach could have been so clearly set out as by this. When we understand that such was our condition by nature, and such was our apostasy from God that there was no way of communicating any good from God to us except by this strange and wonderful way of a Mediator between God and man, we must apprehend that He should obey and suffer and die for us. Certainly there was some mighty difference between God and us and that man's estate was very low. His condition was very desperate or he would not need a remedy such as this. This is that which God would have man to know, what that breach is between Him and their souls. It is such a breach that few think rightly of it. If I should open the law to you with all its curses and set the torments of hell before you, all this could not set out the dreadfulness of the breach between God and you as this point does when I tell you that it was such as requires such a strange and wonderful way of God's being reconciled and pacified towards you.

Secondly, God takes this way because He sees it the most advantageous way for the manifestation of His glory. First the glory of His mercy: there is no way that could have been devised by men or angels to set out the glory of God's mercy in man's salvation as by this way. If God should have said to mankind, "You poor creatures have sinned against Me, but I am merciful and will pardon you," He would have been glorious in this, but now there is infinitely more mercy showed when God says, "You miserable creatures have sinned against Me and such is your condition that, unless the Son of My bosom is made a curse for you, there can be no mercy for you. I am well content that He shall not be spared but shall be given to be a curse to prepare mercy for you." This is glory indeed!

When Christ was born, the angels sang, *Glory to God in the highest*, Luke 2:14. It is as if they had said that this is the highest level of the glory of God in providing such a way of reconciliation with the children of men. God was so set upon this work of showing mercy to mankind that, though it cost the death of His Son, He would have it that way. And that shows it to be the infinite mercy and love indeed, when it breaks through such mighty difficulties. There is the glory of His mercy!

Also, there is more of the glory of His justice. God sets out the glory of His justice here more than if all mankind had been eternally damned. God's justice would not have been honored as much that way as in this way of God's reconciling man unto Himself, and that in these two regards. First, because in Christ, God's justice is glorified actively, whereas, if all men had eternally perished, it would have been a passive glory. It is better to have it glorified actively than passively. As God delights more in active obedience than in passive, so He delights more in the active glory of His justice than in the passive (though there is a kind of activeness in suffering, and so in Christ's sufferings: therefore that distinction of active and passive is needless, for His active obedience was passive and His passive obedience had activity in it).

But God's justice is now glorified perfectly, the debt is fully paid, whereas if all mankind had been damned, the debt would have only been being paid and never have been paid to all eternity. Suppose a poor man owed a thousand pounds and paid two pence a week. He may go on paying it, but cannot pay it if he paid all his life. But now if a rich man comes and lays down the money for him, the debt is paid, and this is a great deal more than if the poor man had kept on paying on a debt he could never pay off. So I say, if all mankind had been damned eternally, God would have had his debt being paid against, but never paid off. But now Christ comes and lays down the payment all at once and asks justice whether it has had enough or not, so that justice is more glorified this way.

The infinite glory of His wisdom appears in reconciling justice and mercy together. That God should be infinitely merciful and just both in one thing is that which no angel in heaven could ever have imagined. Suppose God should have said to all the angels in heaven, "Mankind is in a lost and undone condition, yet I am willing to save him, but only in such a way that I will have infinite mercy and justice reconciled." If all of them had consulted together, they could not possibly have told how this should be. The infinite wisdom of God, and nothing but infinite wisdom could find out such a way as that God should be infinitely merciful and infinitely just, too.

The infiniteness of God's holiness is hereby manifested. If God should have thrown His mercy up and down in the world in a general way, His holiness and hatred of sin would not have appeared as it does now when nothing but sin can expiate sin but the death of His Son. If God should carry any of you to the brink of hell and there let you see all the miseries of the damned, hear all the yelling those under divine wrath, you would say, "O, how God hates sin!" But know this, that in the suffering of Christ there is a greater manifestation of God's hatred for sin than in all the torments of hell!

You who would know how infinitely hateful sin is to God, come and behold Christ, God and man, sweltering under the wrath of His Father. Look upon Him in the garden sweating drops of blood. Come and follow Him to the cross and hear Him cry out in the bitterness of His soul that doleful cry, *My God, My God, why hast Thou forsaken Me?* Behold Jesus Christ, God-man, who was God blessed forever, made a curse for sin and for your sin. Look upon sin in this glass and here see God's hatred of sin.

There are two glasses wherein we see the evil of sin: the bright crystal glass of the law and the red glass of the sufferings of Christ. The latter one more fully, more sensibly, sets out the nature of sin and God's hatred of it. By this you can see the meaning of II Cor.3:18 where the Apostle speaks of the mystery of God, *But we all with open face beholding in a glass the glory of the Lord.* We behold only God's backparts in His works, as God said to Moses. We behold only God's footsteps in His works, but when we behold Him in Christ, we behold Him with open face. What a difference there is in knowing a man when we only see his footprints and when we look him in the face. That's how much difference there is between knowing and His glory as it shines in the works of creation and as it shines in the face of Christ. God will not pardon sin freely as if to say, "You have sinned but I will still pity and pardon you, and that will be the end of it," just to manifest His glory. Though He will pardon sin, He will not do it this way.

A third reason why God brings things about this way is because He saw there could be no such way to draw poor sinners to Himself as this. When God reveals to a sinner that He is not only a merciful God but that He has provided such a strange way to convey His mercy, this has a mighty efficacy to draw the soul to God. For the poor soul, apprehending its own guiltiness, God's hatred of sin, and understanding that the heart of God is set upon such a way of mercy, is, by this mighty argument, prevailed upon to draw near to God in dependence on Him. The soul will argue thusly, "Well, I hear that God, to the end that He might let out mercy to poor sinners, has, of His own infinite wisdom, provided such a strange way of conveyance of this. And when God has made it appear by revealing to me the mystery of the gospel and how His heart is set upon this way of showing mercy to sinners, I conclude that the Lord is willing to be reconciled to me, and why should I be unbelieving any more? Why should I have hard thoughts of God anymore? Why should I remain in my doubting condition any longer?"

You cannot be any more desirous of the salvation of your soul than God is of magnifying His grace and mercy, and God has done more for you than you can possibly do for the salvation of your soul. Besides, it is a mighty argument to draw you, for by this means the infinite distance between God and the soul is taken away. For when the soul sees it has to deal with an infinite Deity that is so far above it, it stands shaking and trembling and does not dare to draw nigh to God. "What have I to do with such a God as this who is so infinitely above me?" says the soul. But now, when you know that Christ is between God and you, then this distance need not scare you. Yea, all your guiltiness, and all the filthiness and pollution of your soul, and all that the law has to say against you, need not be a discouragement to you when you see you have to deal with God and through Jesus Christ.

Therefore, no soul can stand off and say, "How do I know this belongs to me?" Take this one rule: there is nothing which can interest the soul in Christ but Christ Himself. There is no preparation to Christ, but Christ must be all in all. Therefore, do not stand off and ask, "How shall my heart be wrought to these preparations and work thus and thus before I have a part in Christ?" No, do not puzzle yourself about the preparations, but set the mystery of the gospel in this glorious way of God's communicating Himself to you and reconciling man to Himself before your soul. The very efficacy of these truths will have a power upon your heart to draw you to God in this way of reconciliation, and that is the way of true comfort.

The gospel itself, though there is no preparation before, has an efficacy to draw the heart to Christ, for Christ is all in all in that. Do not say, "I am a poor, low creature. I can do nothing. I cannot remember a sermon, I cannot pray or perform any good duty as I ought to do." Remember, soul, Christ is all in all. It is not your weakness, nor the distance between God and you, that hinders you if you rightly apprehend God in Christ reconciling the world to Himself.

Another reason might have been this: God does it to endear His mercy to His saints forever. For indeed, nothing endears God's mercy to them as much as this, that they see it come to them in a way of conveyance. That which will endear mercy to the saints in heaven to all eternity, and for which they shall be full of the praises of God, shall not be so much for the good things they enjoy as for that strange and wonderful way by which they come to enjoy them. This, I say, is that which shall take up the hearts, and be a great part of the work, of the glorified saints in heaven to all eternity: their admiring, adoring, and praising God in Jesus.

God delights to honor His Son. That He might set Him up, He makes Him to be the means of conveying all good to those He intends it. If a king were to honor his son, what way could he take to do it more effectually than to make it so that all the favor he intends to show to anyone can only be through his son? So when God the Father would honor His Son, He appoints from all eternity that all the grace and mercy that any shall have from Him shall only be through His Son. Therefore, as Christ said, *All judgment is committed to the Son, that all men might honor the Son as they honor the Father*. So I may say of the work and dispensation of God's grace that all is conveyed to Christ, and by Him communicated to those who have an interest in Him that the Son might be honored to all eternity.

I shall conclude in a few words of application to work upon that which has been said.

First, if it be thus, let us stand awhile and admire the depths of the counsel of God and the infinite glory of the riches of His grace to mankind that God should ever have such thoughts towards such poor worms as we are; that He should not rather have let such despicable creatures eternally perish than go in such a strange way to show mercy to them. Truly, brethren,

God has done more in bringing a poor soul to Himself than in creating heaven and earth. The work of creating heaven and earth is only a low piece of work in comparison to this wonderful way of conveying grace and mercy to the children of men through His Son. This is the masterpiece of all the works that God has ever done or ever will do, and therefore He is to be admired and adored in this.

We are to glorify God in every creature, but how is God to be glorified in His Son, then, wherein so much of His glory already appears? If it is a sin for us not to sanctify the name of God when we behold His glory in His lowliest works, oh, what a sin it is not to sanctify the name of God in beholding the mystery of the gospel and His shining in the face of Jesus Christ! God expects that those who live under the gospel should spend their days and their thoughts and their talk about the glory which He has manifested in His Son. Oh, you who have such light, drossy spirits, who can spend your precious thoughts upon such poor things as you do, know that here is an Object to take up your thoughts, and your sin is abundantly the greater in this: that you spend your thoughts about such vanities when God sets before you so glorious an Object to raise up your hearts unto Himself. You that spend a great deal of your lives in vanity, know that this day you have heard a truth that, above all things in the world, should take up your time and thoughts in contemplating it.

You that have more time and estates than others

and are not put upon to get your bread as others are, and so have greater opportunities for the worship and service of God, instead of searching into this truth, you spend your time in vanity and light things as if there were no greater matters to take up your hearts! It is a sign of a vain and frothy spirit that when God propounds such glorious things to you, your souls should be content to baffle out your time in vanity and things that will not profit. If you seek evidence for your souls that Christ is all in all to you and shall be for all eternity, look to this: if God has ever opened your eyes to see His glory in the mystery of the gospel and your heart is taken with it and overcome by it, it is an argument that you are indeed the soul which God has received to mercy in His Christ. But, says the Apostle, II Cor.4:3, *if our gospel be hid, it is hid to them that are lost.*

There are a great many to whom the gospel is preached, and yet it is hidden to them. And it is hidden to you if you speak of Christ only in a formal way and think it enough to say, "I hope to be saved by God in Jesus Christ." But do you see that in the gospel which raises your heart with admiration and that darkens all the glory of the world? Do you see more of the glory of God shining in that one sentence, *For God so loved the world that He gave His only begotten Son, that whosoever believes in Him, should not perish, but have everlasting life* than you see in the whole frame of the creation of heaven and earth? You hope, you say, to go to heaven. But what would you do there? The work of saints and angels in heaven joined together is to magnify God for this great work of His. Then begin the work here and give God the glory for the great things He has done for the children of men.

The second use is this: if Christ is all in all, then let us bless God that ever we knew Christ, and that the great mystery of the gospel has been revealed to us. For otherwise we would have been without God in the world, and what would have become of us had not this grace of God in the gospel been revealed to us? Could it ever have entered into your heart? Certainly not, nor into the heart of any creature in heaven and earth. Therefore, blessed are your ears that hear the things you hear. Blessed are your eyes which see the things you see, and know that when you come to live under the ministry of the gospel, you enjoy the greatest mercy that you have enjoyed since you were born.

Coming under a powerful ministry that reveals Christ and brings the day of salvation to the soul is none other than the fruit of prayer of Jesus Christ for that soul. Compare Is.49:8 with II Cor.6:1-2 and you shall see this. Is.49:8 says, *Thus saith the Lord, in an acceptable time have I heard thee, and in a day of salvation I helped thee.* Now it is apparent by the context that this is to be understood of Christ, that God the Father here speaks to His Son. Well, what is this acceptable time and day of salvation in which Christ is heard? Look at II Cor.6, verses 1 and 2. In the chapter before, Paul had told them that they were ambassadors for Christ. *We then as workers together with God, beseech you also that ye receive not the grace of God in vain.* What is this grace of God? It is the ministry of the gospel, *for he saith I have heard thee in a time accepted,* and mark how he applies it, *behold now is the accepted time, now is the day of salvation.* It is as if he should say, "The acceptable time and day of salvation in which God the Father has heard Christ is now. Now that we, the ambassadors of Christ, have come and opened the mystery of the gospel to you, now is the time wherein God the Father hears the Son for you."

What a mercy is this! What an engagement upon you that, when you hear anything of the mystery of the gospel opened to you, you are to look upon it as the fruit of the prayer of Jesus Christ. So when God sends a faithful minister to any congregation, it is the fruit of the prayer of Christ. Christ prays to the Father that there might be an acceptable time for such a people, for such a man and woman. It may be that they have gone a long time in ignorance and profaneness, aye, but Christ has been praying to the Father for them and, when this acceptable time comes, then God disposes of them. This man shall go out of such a wicked family and shall live in a godly family or shall come to hear a sermon. There he shall hear the wonderful things of the gospel opened to him and shall come to understand this great mystery of God's letting Himself out through Christ to His people. There the Lord will renew him by a work of grace and bring his heart over to Himself. This is the acceptable time when God reveals the mystery of the gospel to any soul. Therefore, bless

God for this.

Thirdly, this shows how dear Jesus Christ should be to us. Oh, how we should delight and take contentment in Him who brings the treasuries of grace from the bosom of the Father and opens them to us. And He not only opens the mind of God the Father to us, but comes and lets out the treasure of God's goodness to us. It was stopped before, but Christ opens the floodgates and lets the current of grace and mercy in upon us. Oh, how dear, then, should Christ be to us?

It was the speech of that martyr, Master Lambert, "None but Christ, none but Christ." Yea, when he suffered martyrdom for Christ, then none but Christ was dear to him because he saw that Christ was the way of conveying all good to him. If God were now to make a man the means of conveying a great deal of good to a nation, every man will be ready to have his eye upon that man. But there was never such a way of conveying good to us as Christ. Therefore, how should our hearts love Him, prize Him, and rejoice at the very thought of Him?

If you have a dear friend, and God makes that friend an instrument of mercy to you, how does it endear you to that friend? If the husband is an instrument of good to his wife or the wife to her husband, if a minister to his people or people to their minister? And so it is in all relations. When we can look upon others as a means of conveying God's mercy to us, it is a mighty argument to knit our hearts unto them, and indeed this is the way to obtain love. It may be the wife complains that her husband does not love her or the husband complains that his wife does not love him. Why, now, be as instrumental as you can to convey the goodness of God to them, and this will mightily endear and knit them to you. And if it does so between man and man, how should it do so much more between us and Christ, who is indeed the Husband of His church, and through whom the fulness of God is let out to His people? Oh, how dear and precious, therefore, ought He to be to us!

Fourthly, is Christ all in all? Then if we have an interest in Him, it should satisfy and content us though we have nothing or though we are nothing. Why? Because if we have Christ we have all. Though you lack parts, friends, estates, outward comforts, know Christ is to be your all, and is He not enough? As He said, *Am I not better to thee than ten sons?* So Christ says to the soul, "What do you lack? You lack this comfort and the other comfort, but am I not all in all to you, and better than all?" Yea, be willing to be made nothing, for all is made up in Christ.

Again, it should have put us upon this, to be willing to give up all we have to Christ. Alas, our all is but a poor all, yet give it to Christ. Our parts, our estates, our names, let Christ have all because He is our all.

Let Him be the rule of our prizing things. As far as we see anything of Christ, prize it suitably. It is reported of Master Bucer that if he could see anything of Christ in any man or woman, though they were never so poor and mean, his heart would close with them. It is said of Austin that before his conversion he took great delight in reading Cicero's works, but afterward he said, "I did not find the name of Christ in all of Cicero," and that took his heart off of him. So in all you enjoy, look how much you see of Christ in it. So far let your delight and esteem be carried out towards it and no farther.

With what mighty intention of spirit should the heart be put forth towards Jesus Christ in all things! Though God gives you an estate and honor in the world, if you have not Christ you have nothing. You have not that which makes way for you to eternity. Therefore, do not be satisfied with anything without Christ. As Abraham said, *What wilt Thou give me Lord, seeing I go childless?* So you say, "Lord, You have given me a portion in this world. You have given me credit and reputation among men, but, Lord, what is all this to me if I go Christless and do not have Him that is the conveyance of grace to my soul, Him that is all in all? Oh, Lord, You have taught me this day that such is the distance and breach between You and me that, unless it is made up through a Mediator, I must eternally perish. Therefore, give me Christ, whatever else You deny me."

Do not satisfy yourselves with anything without Christ! Many hypocrites satisfy themselves with gifts. If they have gifts, then they are content. Consider that parable in Matt. 13:45-46, *The merchant man sought after goodly pearls, but when he had found the pearl of price, then he went and sold all that he had and bought it.* Now gifts and parts and other achievements are these goodly pearls, but Christ is the Pearl of price. Therefore, whatever you have, be willing to part with it for Him. If God has revealed to you the Pearl of price, let no goodly pearls satisfy you. Many souls perish eternally because they are satisfied with goodly pearls and do not endeavor to obtain this Pearl of price. In your seeking God, be sure to take Christ along with you.

I will give you just this note: if it were your last time to pray to God and your everlasting estate depended on God's mercy, should you seek God never so earnestly, if it is only in a natural way as your Creator, your condition would be very dreadful and you would perish eternally. If God should lay any of you upon your sick or death beds and you should cry to God for mercy, be sure to take Christ along with you and look upon God through Christ, or else all your cries will be of no avail. Luther said that God, looked upon outside of Christ, is most dreadful and terrible. And it proves a great deal of ignorance in us when we think we can go to God and find mercy in Him without considering Him as a God that will be reconciled to us only through His Son.

To conclude all, as Christ says, *If I be lifted up, I will draw all men unto Me.* So this is the work of our ministry. We have spent time among you so that we might labor to lift up Christ to you and, oh, that God would be pleased to draw all your souls to Himself.

SERMON 3

"...now faith is the substance of things hoped for,
the evidence of things not seen..."
(Hebrews 11:6)

In the latter end of the former chapter, the Apostle exhorts us to perseverance and shows the great evil and danger of drawing back. Now to the end that evil might be prevented, he shows what it is that will deliver us from it. Whatever others do, or whatever temptations or afflictions we meet with to draw us back, the just still shall live by faith: *Now faith is the substance of things hoped for, the evidence of things not seen.*

In this chapter he falls upon this argument, to wit, the opening of the doctrine and practice of faith. The words read are an excellent description of faith, though not an exact definition of it, *the substance of things hoped for, the evidence of things not seen.* The word in the original translated "substance" has many significations: the fundamental, the foundation of things hoped for, the subsistence, the substantiality of things hoped for; those things that in themselves have no real present subsistence to us but are things to come, and they are hoped for. But faith gives them a present, real, substantial being to us.

The word translated "evidence" is a logical term, and signifies such a kind of conviction, as is by way of dispute and clear demonstration, that it compels one to yield to it. That is the proper meaning of the word, that, although the objects of faith are things not seen, either by the eye of sense or the eye of reason, yet faith brings such a light with it and makes them so demonstratively clear, that it even forces the soul to a belief of them so that it has the fullest conviction of them that can possibly be.

Two things are here said of faith: first, that it gives a substantial, real, present being to things hoped for; and second, that it is the evidence of things not seen. In the first of these, we have these two things: first, that there are many glorious things which the saints hope for that they do not yet have. They are men of hopes. Secondly, that their faith gives a real and substantial being to those things for which they hope.

In the second of these we have, likewise, two things: first, that the things of God are not seen and, secondly, that faith is the evidence of those things that are not seen.

There are great things that the saints hope for that they do not yet have. They are men of hopes. They hope that before long they shall be delivered from all sin and sorrows; that they shall never more sin, never more be tempted, never more suffer, never more fear. They hope that the time is coming when it shall be said of all their sins, as Moses said of the Egyptians, Exodus 14:13, "Your enemies that now you see, you shall never see them again." They hope that these vile bodies of theirs, these bodies of clay, bodies of vileness, bodies of sin, shall before long be made glorious bodies; that these pieces of dirt shall, within a while, shine more gloriously than the sun in the firmament.

They hope that the image of God shall be perfected in them before long so that they shall be fully united to God and shall be made one with the Father, as the Father and the Son are one.

They hope that they shall meet with their blessed Saviour in the air and with their eyes behold Him coming in His glory. They hope that they shall possess those glorious mansions which He has gone ahead to prepare for them. They hope that their eyes shall be blessed with a glorious vision of the Deity, that they shall see God, and so see Him as to be like Him. They hope that they shall enjoy full communion with the Lord, that they shall have the immediate and full lettings out of a Deity into their souls and bodies without any intermission. They hope that they shall join with the blessed angels and saints in eternal hallelujahs and shall be everlastingly admiring and adoring the name of the great God for those eternal mysteries of redemption by Christ. They hope that they shall keep a perpetual and eternal Sabbath and shall no more be encumbered with natural things, with the things of the earth, but shall have perfect and everlasting rest in Christ, and shall live in God as in an infinite ocean of excellency.

They hope for these things, but are these not conceits? Are they not notions, pretty, fine fancies with which they please themselves? Is there any reality in these things?

Indeed, if these things were real and substantial, if there were as great a reality and as much substance in the things they hope for as there is in the things they enjoy in the world presently, if they could see them as certainly as they see the things that are before their eyes, it would be something.

Well, says the Apostle, there is a principle to make all these things substantial to you, and faith is the substance of things hoped for. These hopes are not conceits and notions, they are raised up in their hearts by the mighty power of the Holy Ghost, Romans 15:13, *Now the God of hope fill you with all joy and peace in believing, that you may abound in hope through the power of the Holy Ghost.* The power of the Holy Ghost is not needed to raise fancies and conceits in men's hearts, but the hopes of the saints are such as are raised by the power of the Holy Ghost. God Himself is styled by their hopes, *now the God of hope.* God is not the God of fancies and conceits, He is the God of the hopes of His saints.

These hopes are given to them so that they might be kept from drawing back and might be upheld in whatever they suffer. Therefore, the Scriptures compare our hope to an anchor and to a helmet. You know that of all dangers, these are the greatest: shipwreck by sea or enemies by land. Our hope is to help us against both. Against dangers by sea, by shipwreck, our hope is an anchor; against dangers by land, by enemies, our hope is a helmet.

For the present, the hope of the saints is as the cork to the net that keeps it from sinking to the bottom. Though they may be in the water, and the lead of their troubles and afflictions may be weighing them down, their hope keeps them above water. They have great hopes and they have that which makes their hopes substantial, for their faith is the substance of things hoped for.

That is the second thing I now come to: carnal hearts think there is no substantial, real excellency in anything except in the outward excellencies of the world. They think that money, lands, honors, and the pleasures and delights of the flesh have substance in them, and that there is something of reality in these. Now I beseech you, observe the difference between the judgment of the Holy Ghost and the judgment of a carnal heart. Whereas a carnal heart looks upon outward things as the only substantial things (therefore you call rich men "substantial" men, and the Scripture, speaking in the language of men, calls a man's estate his substance, because men count their estate their substance), the Holy Ghost accounts all those things that the world looks upon as substances to be only mere conceits (and those that judge according to the Holy Ghost do likewise).

You know, St. John reckons all things in the world in three ranks: profits, pleasures, or honors; the lusts of the flesh, the pride of life, and the delight of the eye. That which the world counts as their greatest substance, their riches and their estates, the Holy Ghost thinks of in the following terms, Prov.23:4-5, *Labor not to be rich, cease from thine own wisdom: wilt thou set thine eyes upon that which is not?* That which you call your substance, the Holy Ghost says is not, it has no being at all.

Well, you say, honors and preferments have something in them. No, they have nothing in them either. Acts 25:23 says, *Agrippa and Bernice came in great pomp to the judgment seat,* glittering in their brave apparel, but the words translated "great pomp" literally mean that they came with much fancy. What greater honor is there than for princes to come to the judgment seat in their robes, glittering before the eyes of their objects? Thus they did, and yet their great glory, in the judgment of the Holy Ghost, was only a great fancy.

Regarding the lusts of the flesh, in Amos 6:5-6 you have the sensuality of the people set out very fully, *They lie upon beds of ivory, and stretch themselves upon their couches, and eat the lambs out of the flock, and the calves out of the midst of the stall; they chant to the sound of the viol, and invent to themselves instruments of music; they drink wine in bowls,* and in verse 13, it all comes to this, *Ye rejoice in a thing of naught.* That is, that which has nothing in it. There is no reality, no substantial excellency in any of these things, neither in riches, honors, or pleasures. But mark how the Holy Ghost judges spiritual things. What substance is there in them, which are only conceits to carnal hearts.

Wisdom says, in Prov. 8:20-21, *I lead in the way of righteousness, that I may cause those that love me to inherit substance,* to inherit that which is. Tremelius translates it "as if nothing had a being but that which wisdom causes to inherit." And Hebrews 10:33-34, *You were made a gazing stock both by reproaches and afflictions, and took joyfully the spoiling of your goods.* But mark how this came to pass, *knowing in yourselves that ye have in heaven a better, and an enduring substance.* So that which was only a conceit and a notion to the world, by faith they saw to be substantial. In Hebrews 11:10, it is said that Abraham looked for a city with foundations. There was no city in the world that had foundations in Abraham's eyes except the city that he looked for, and it was his faith that gave the city foundations.

Thus we see the differing judgments of the Holy Ghost and the world. While we live upon the earth, we think the earth is very great, and the sun, moon, and stars to be only little things, for so they seem to us. But were we in heaven, we would then see the sun and moon and stars to be great and vast bodies, and the earth to be only a point by comparison. While men have earthly hearts, they look upon the things of heaven as conceits, as poor, small, inconsiderable things not worth looking after. But if by divine principles they were just once lifted up to heaven and could converse there, then they would see the things of heaven to be great matters and the things here below to be only poor, low, inferior things not worth minding or affecting. Those things that are the objects of faith are substantial things, and faith gives them that substance.

And they are substantial things, first, because they have in them more than appears to be in them. We count as substantial that which has more in it than appears. Those things that make a great show and do not have that in them which they make a show of, we count as vain and without substance. A piece of cloth that does not have that in it which it shows, we say that it has no substance in it.

Now the things of God have abundantly more in them than they show and, therefore, they are substantial. Hence it is that when Christ shall come in His glory, II Thess.1:10, *He shall be admired in all them that believe.* They see a great deal of excellency in Christ and they love Him, and their hearts are towards Him for what they see in Him now. But hereafter, He shall appear abundantly more glorious than they thought. Then they shall say, "Indeed, we saw much excellency in Christ, but now we see infinitely more glory and excellency than we ever imagined."

Secondly, the things of heaven that are the objects of faith are substantial because there is most of God in them. God is the infinite First Being of all and gives being to all. Therefore, that which has most of the First Being in it must be the most substantial and real good. Though it is true that all creatures are filled with God's excellencies, spiritual and heavenly things are most filled with God. The very nature of God is in them and there is the very life of God and the image and glory of God, and there God especially communicates Himself. God has two ways of communication: one is to His

Son, and that is in an infinite way that we do not understand; and the other is to His creatures. His special communication of Himself to His creatures is in spiritual and heavenly things. Therefore, they must be the most substantial and real things to the soul.

And then thirdly, they are substantial things and not notions and conceits because they are the very center of the thoughts and intentions of God Himself, and that at which He aims in all His works towards His creatures, and the very center of the most excellent creatures that God ever made. That which is the very issue of the great design of God in making the world, and of all the works He does in the world, and the highest good any creature is capable of, is certainly no conceit but has a great deal of substantial being in it. The good we have in spiritual and heavenly things is the very issue of God's design from all eternity in His full communion of Himself to His creature, and it is the highest good any creature is capable of. Therefore, spiritual things are real and substantial.

They are real and substantial things because we find they have a real and substantial operation upon the souls of those who are acquainted with them. Oh, the mighty work that appears upon the hearts of the godly from the apprehension of spiritual things that are the objects of faith! How do spiritual things tune and raise the hearts of men that previously were low, base, drossy, and vile, to converse with God in the highest way and kind that it is possible for a creature to converse with God! What great things do they enable the soul to do! Those things that have such a substantial operation must be real and substantial.

Lastly, they have an eternal subsistence that shall never vanish or fade away. When all other things shall wither as the grass, spiritual and heavenly things shall abide forever. Therefore, they are the only substantial things.

But, then, as they are thus in themselves, how do they come to be thus to the soul? It is by faith! Faith gives them the bottom, the foundation, the substantiality of their being. And I note this, rather, because the great reason why our hearts are not taken with spiritual things is because we do not see into the reality and substance that is in them.

Now faith gives spiritual things their substantial being. First, because it is faith that carries the soul to contemplate God Himself and enables the soul to discern the excellency and glory that there is in God, to know much of God in His own essence and being. It elevates the soul to converse with God in a higher way than reason can do (though it is true that a great deal of God is understood by reason). By faith, the soul comes to know what riches there are in these excellent and glorious things of God. It first sees them in God, and then it sees this God to be infinitely willing to communicate and let Himself out to His creature. Then, by faith, the soul converses with the deep and glorious counsels of God between Himself and His Son. It sees into the great design God had in sending His Son into the world to work and bring to pass those high and glorious intentions He had in communicating Himself to the children of men through a Mediator.

Faith converses with the great things of the covenant of grace and there sees into the unsearchable riches that have no footsteps in the creature. That is what the word signifies. We cannot see them by reason or by the creature. A special object which faith works on is the covenant of grace in the gospel, and it sees the riches that are revealed there.

Faith receives the testimony of the Holy Ghost. The Holy Ghost is appointed by the Father and the Son to witness these great things, to manifest to the soul the deep things of God. Those things that are only mere notions otherwise to the heart of a man are revealed to the soul by the Spirit of God. Faith works on these objects and closes with them as the proper sphere to move in. Faith makes all those glorious things that are revealed concerning the happiness of those to whom God intends eternal good, real and substantial to the soul, such things as the soul can build on, such things as the soul can dare venture itself and its eternal estate on. We need to have a good foundation in those things upon which we venture our eternal state. And because it must be the work of faith to have such apprehensions of the gospel, to be willing to venture its eternal condition upon it, therefore it needs to have a sure foundation. Hence, faith is the substance of things hoped for and gives a real being unto those things.

As it makes them real and substantial, so there is another thing included in this word. It makes them present. Though they are things hoped for, by faith they still have a present subsistence to the soul. They are looked upon by faith as now subsisting though, in themselves, they do not. Faith partakes much of the nature of God. It has a kind of omnipotent power in it to create something out of nothing. There are many excellent works of faith, and this is a special one: to give a being to that which in itself has none, to make it a substantial, real being to the soul.

The work of faith in this is very observable. For evil things that are very close, faith can make them be at a mighty distance. For good things that are never so far off, faith can make them be at hand. Observe what the Scripture says of this, first regarding evils that are very nigh and encompass us round about: when we are in the midst of them, faith can put the evil at a distance. As in Psalm 91:7, *A thousand shall fall at thy side, and ten thousand at thy right hand, but it shall not come nigh thee; not come nigh thee.* If he had said, "it shall not come upon thee," it would have been one thing, but to say, *it shall not come nigh thee,* this is a strange kind of expression. How could it be said not to come nigh him when thousands fell on both hands and he was in the midst of it? It was by faith. Faith put that at a distance which was right upon him.

The strength of reason will help one when the plague is a great way off. Then a man thinks he is safe enough because he is far enough from it. But suppose the plague comes into your house, into your chamber. Then to believe the promise that it shall not come nigh to you is a mighty work of faith. Faith puts present evils at a a great distance. Then, on the other side, for things that are absent or a great way off, faith can make them as if they were really subsisting. Therefore, Hebrews 11:13 says of the fathers that they saw the promises afar off and embraced them. The word in the original says that they saluted the promises. When friends salute each other, they must be nigh to each other. Their faith made the promises which were a great way off to be with them as if they were present. Therefore, it is said of Abraham that he saw Christ's day and rejoiced.

The Scripture speaks of taking hold of eternal life, and we do that by faith. The Scripture speaks of being in heaven, *receiving the end of your faith*. It is not "you shall receive," but *you are now receiving*. Psalm 108: 7-8 says, *God hath spoken in His holiness, I will rejoice, I will divide Sechem...Gilead is mine, Manasseth is mine.* Mark it, *is mine,* he concludes, as if the things were already done, for it was so by faith. Faith gives a present subsistence to things.

Reason itself has a great deal of power to make things that are future to be present, both in evil things and in good. In evil things, a man who is a contemplative man and has a wicked heart will fetch the sweetness of his lust and sin which is a great way off and make it present by meditation. He rolls it up and down in his thoughts and so acts his sin contemplatively, though he may be in hell before he really acts it. As reason and discourse can fetch in a lust and make it as if it were present, so reason can go a great way in making a future good thing as if it were present.

This is the difference between a rational creature and a sensual one. A sensual creature is only for the things that are before it, but reason can fetch things that are absent and make them present. In regard of this, God has a mighty advantage over mankind, either for the bringing of His wrath on them or for bestowing happiness upon them. As you can fetch in your lusts that are absent and make them as present to you in your thoughts by the work and discourse of reason so, by the work of this faculty, God can make evils and plagues, though future, to be as present with you. And in this respect, the woeful evils of those that perish eternally may be set out dreadfully. They, being reasonable creatures by the work of their reason, may fetch in all the misery that they shall endure to eternity, to fill up every moment's misery, that all the misery they shall endure to eternity they shall possess presently and together. Therefore, the torment of a brute creature is infinitely short of a reasonable creature.

Suppose a brute beast were in hell. Its misery would still come infinitely short of a man's, because a brute creature apprehends no more misery than what it is undergoing at that instant. But now, if a reasonable creature is in torment and knows it shall be eternally, by thought and discourse it can fetch into that very instant all the pain it must endure forever.

So it is regarding happiness: those that are saved

shall be infinitely happy every moment because they shall fetch in all the happiness they shall have to eternity to make them happy every moment. This is the work of reason. Now if reason can make future things to be as present, how much more can faith, which is not only reason elevated but is a principle higher than reason?

A man who despairs brings hell to himself before he is in hell, and makes the hell that is absent to be as if it were present. Hence, some in their despairing have cried out that they were in hell. Francis Spira said he was in hell and hellfire was upon him because, by despair, that which is future has a real kind of subsistence in the heart of a man as if it were now present. As despair brings in the reality of God's wrath that is future and makes it as if it were present, so faith brings in the reality of God's love and mercy that is to come and makes it as if it were present. It is as genuine a work of faith to make future things present as any work of faith. Now I should have shown you in what respects faith makes things present that are to come and what the work of faith in them is, but briefly, it makes all things present that are to come.

First, faith makes all things present that are to come because it sees all things as certainly as if they were already. If a man has a bond for one hundred pounds that he is sure of, he says he has a hundred pounds because of the certainty of it.

Secondly, faith makes all things present because faith looks upon the possession of things, that not only they shall be but that now there is a possession of them, and that in two ways. First, Christ our head has gone before to prepare mansions for us and, in our name, to take possession of heaven. Therefore, we have taken possession in our Head. Secondly, we have the first fruits of the Spirit, the first fruits of the glorious things of heaven and, in that regard, we have taken possession ourselves, and therefore they are as if they were present to faith. Thirdly, there is such an infiniteness in eternity that the time still to go before we take full possession is not considerable. Therefore, faith looks on them as if they were present.

Fourthly, faith eyes the things of heaven continually, and they are therefore present because they are always in the eyes of faith. Fifthly, the "presentness" of them is seen in this because the saints enjoy all in God, for this is the happiness of heaven to see all the glory and blessedness of God. Now faith does something of this here. Faith enables us to see great things in God. The enjoyment of communion with God for the present, the beholding of heaven in God and seeing all things in Him, must make a present, real subsistence of them to the soul. Thus I have spoken briefly of faith's being the substance of things hoped for.

Now for the use: if faith is the substance of things hoped for and gives being to things as high and glorious as the things of God are, then certainly faith itself must be a very substantial thing. Faith is not a conceit and a notion, for it gives reality and substantial being to those things the world counts as conceits. Faith is the most substantial, glorious thing in the world. It is in the working of faith that the power of God appears more than anything in the world. Therefore, in Eph. 1:19-20, there are some six or seven gradations of the wonderful power of God that appear in the working of faith. Now that must be an exceedingly substantial thing that has such a mighty power of God working in it. God does not usually put forth extraordinary power to do ordinary things.

When He speaks of faith, He sets out His power in a glorious manner and in an extraordinary way, and thereby tells us that faith has some great matter in it. And, indeed, faith has much in it. Though it is a grace that empties us of ourselves, yet it is that whereby the believer is enabled to do one of the most glorious works that a poor creature was ever able to do. For a poor soul to see itself in its own filth, under sin and guilt, and to see the wrath of an infinite Deity incensed against it; to see the infinite justice of God requiring satisfaction and the infinite holiness of God hating sin; to have the accusations of conscience, of Satan, of the world and, being sensible of this, still to lay hold of a Mediator between God and man; to trust in a righteousness beyond itself and to offer it up to God the Father for a full atonement and satisfaction; to venture itself and its eternal estate upon it; being unholy and filthy in itself, still to unite itself to God in as close a union as a creature can possible have with the Creator (the hypostatic union of the human nature of Christ with the divine), for faith to be able to do this is a high and most glorious work, and there is an abundance of the power of God appearing in it.

By this we may discover the vanity of the faith of the greatest number of people in the world, who have nothing but mere emptiness in them. Their very faith is only a notion, and it is no wonder, then, if all things they believe are only notions. They can do nothing with their faith. You say you hope and believe and trust in God's mercy, but what can you do with your faith? What real substantial work of faith is upon your hearts? When faith comes, there comes the mighty power of God and His wonderful glory into the soul. That creates and gives substantial being to the mighty, high, and glorious objects in the world. Therefore, know that faith is not a dead, slight, empty thing in the soul, but it has a mighty operation upon the hearts of men and women, and certainly that faith that must save a soul must have high and glorious operations in the soul.

If faith gives a substantial being to things hoped for, then we must learn to strengthen and exercise our faith in the things we hope for. Which of us does not hope for great and glorious things? Let faith be exercised and strengthened in these things. If all those blessed things we spoke of were present to the soul, O how our hearts would be above the creature. How we would look upon all things here below as dung, filth, dross! How would our spirits be taken up in wondering at the glory of God that appears in those things! How would our hearts be enflamed with love to God!

How would our conversations be in heaven for the present! What heavenly thoughts and heavenly affections would be in all our ways! And how would we venture to go through fire and water for God, to do anything, to suffer anything, be anything for God.

If our faith makes such glorious things as these real and substantial to us, how substantial would our duties and services be! Why is it, then, that our duties have so much vanity in them, are so empty, having nothing but circumstance in them? If our faith gives a subsistence to such blessed and glorious things of eternal life, it will likewise give a subsistence to all our duties and services so that we do not offer to God empty and dead services. Consider this, you who, though you do not dare omit duties, offer empty duties to God. Your works should be the works of faith, and faith should give them such a subsistence equal to your hopes. Therefore, do not satisfy yourselves with that faith which will not give a subsistence to your duties, and do not think it will give a subsistence to such glorious things as we have spoken of. This much for the first particular, *faith is the substance of things hoped for*. Now I will speak a little of the second, *it is the evidence of things not seen*.

There are two things here. First, that the things of grace, spiritual and heavenly things, are not seen. Secondly, faith gives an evidence to those things. The Apostle says in Gal. 5:19-22 that the works of the flesh are manifest. But when he comes to the works of the Spirit, he says that the works of the Spirit are these. He does not say that they are manifest, for indeed they are things that are not seen. It is true that the operations of them may appear, but there is no external work of grace that a hypocrite may not do. Therefore, the works of the Spirit cannot be said to be seen either by the eye of sense or reason.

For the things of heaven, the Apostle says, II Cor. 2:18, *While we look not at the things which are seen, but at the things which are not seen, for the things which are seen are temporal, but the things which are not seen are eternal.* I might here reveal to you how it comes to pass that spiritual and heavenly things are not seen by sense and reason. I thought of many arguments to give you to reveal this, but I will only draw out two or three particulars. The riches of a Christian in spiritual and heavenly things are like the riches of the sea. It may be that outwardly you see nothing but hideous waves and a great deal of filth, but the riches are at the bottom, and the riches of the earth are within and hidden. They do not appear. So the riches of a Christian are things not seen. They are things that are in the very bosom of God, in the very heart of God. Now as no man knows the things of a man but the spirit of man, so no man knows the things of God but the Spirit of God and him to whom God reveals them.

They are things that are beyond the principles of reason. They are too high, and so they are too glorious for such a faculty as reason. If an object is too glorious for sense, it destroys sense. So these objects are too high for reason and therefore cannot be seen by reason.

The blindness of a man naturally is such that he cannot see these things. Chiefly, God so orders things in His providence that He goes quite contrarily to that which He has promised regarding sense and reason. It is the way of God to hide His glorious excellencies by seeming to go in the ways of providence directly contrary to what He has promised. We might show how God has hidden His mercy to His own people from sense and reason. The example of Abraham is worth considering. There were two promises God made to Abraham: one about going out of his own country and carrying him to a land flowing with milk and honey; the other, that He would make his seed to be as the stars of heaven, and that in his seed all the nations of the earth would be blessed.

Mark it now. If Abraham had not had something to prove that which was not seen, he could never have seen the faithfulness of God in these promises, for when he had left his own country he came to Canaan, the land which had been promised. But as soon as he was there, he was ready to starve, ready to fly to Egypt. If he had not had faith, he would have fallen off and would have been ready to turn back.

Then for the second promise, that in his seed *all the nations of the earth should be blessed.* Abraham lived seventy years and his wife had no child. It was no longer possible for her to have a child, for she was old and Abraham's body was dead. Then, after she bore a child, he was ordered to kill him. Isaac, being saved, must be forty years old before he can get married, and, when he is married, he can have no children for twenty years. So in the first one hundred and fifty years after the promise, there were only seventy of Abraham's seed, yet the promise was that in his seed all the nations of the earth should be blessed. Thus, God seems to go contrary to what He had promised.

Jacob is also an example. God commanded Jacob to return from Laban, and after that, mark how God follows him. First, his uncle Laban follows him with thoughts to slay him. Secondly, in his journey his wife's nurse dies. Thirdly, his wife dies. Fourthly, Dinah is ravished. Fifthly, his two sons, Simeon and Levi, commit the villainous act that makes him stink in the nostrils of the people of the land. Sixth, Esau comes to destroy him, and all this happened in the journey that God commanded Jacob to take. Now if Jacob had not had faith to look through these things to the things that might encourage him in his way, it would have been impossible for him to go on.

When God brought Israel to Canaan, you know what they went through in the wilderness. When they came to Canaan, a land flowing with milk and honey, God brought them to the worst part of it. The south part was the hottest, driest, most barren part of the country. Thus, God seemed to act in contrary ways, and this hides the excellency of the things of God. Hence it comes to pass that they are not seen. The things of God are not seen by a carnal eye and require more than reason to apprehend them.

First, it makes us stop wondering that men of excellent parts and reason do not see the things of God but rather slight them. Do not be offended by this, they are things not seen. It is a great deceit in many, who think that because such and such men have larger abilities of reason than others do to understand natural things, that it must follow that they have deeper apprehensions of spiritual things. Men reason thusly, "What, you poor, simple men and women understand these things when there are great scholars and learned men that do not see them?" This argues a carnal heart! As if the strength of reason could make men apprehend more than faith can.

You know what Christ said, *Father, I thank Thee that Thou hast hid these things from the wise and prudent and hast revealed them to babes,* Matt.11:25. Notwithstanding such expressions from Christ, we see the temper of the men of the world. Alas, they look upon religion as a most foolish and ridiculous thing. When one man sees another man very earnest about a thing he considers inconsequential, he cannot help but think of him as foolish. When the men of the world see the people of God fervent and zealous about things in which they see no excellency, and see them willing to venture and suffer them, they count this as folly and madness.

When Christ, in danger of His life, John 18:37-38, tells Pilate that He came into the world to bear witness to the truth, Pilate asked, "What is truth?" He said that in a slight way, as if he had said, "You come here to answer for Your life, and You need to take care of that! Why do you talk of truth when Your life is in question?" When carnal men see others venture their estates and lives for poor, trivial things (as they always seem to do), they count this as folly. Why do they do so? Because the things of God are not seen. Therefore, in spiritual and heavenly things we must always endeavor to beat down reason and to advance faith. Luther said, "In the things of God we must not be continually asking the reason, for they are the things that are not seen. Faith kills the beast of reason in spiritual things." Reason, kept under faith, has a good use, but it is as a beast to be slain so that we may see more of spiritual things.

There is a story told about a company of bishops who gathered together. There was a philosopher with them who disputed the Christian faith. He argued so keenly that the bishops were unable to respond. There was a godly man there, however, a poor, weak man who desired the liberty to dispute that which they were unable to dispute. Though at first they were afraid he would spoil the cause because of his weakness, at length they gave him permission to speak. He propounded certain principles of religion to the philosopher and said to him, "Do you believe these things?" He said no more, only "Do you believe these things?" Upon that, the philosopher yielded.

There are many who are sure that Christ died for them, that their sins are pardoned, and that they are children of God They endeavor to make this out by arguments from the effects, and would try themselves by such and such notes. But we should rather, and in the first place, go the way the Apostle does here: we believe and are sure. We should cast our souls upon the truth of the Word and, by believing, come to be sure. So much for the first, that the things of God are things not seen.

Now for faith, that evidences and makes them clear, *We know in whom we have believed,* II Tim. 1:12, and the mercies of God in Christ are called *the sure mercies of David,* Acts 13:34. Faith is not a mere notion, imagination, or conceit, but it is that which makes all sure and certain to the soul. I should answer a case here, whether or not there may not be faith without assurance, that is, without assurance of a man's own salvation by Christ.

Certainly it must be a great mistake to put that upon the being of faith which is the riches of faith, for so the Scripture calls assurance. A man may be able to carry on his trade though he is not rich, and a man may be a believer though he is not rich in assurance. Now assurance is the cream of faith, the riches of faith. I should also show how far faith can be an evidence where there is doubting. The assurance we have by faith, building upon the word and drawing conclusions from divine principles, is enough evidence that the soul can venture upon it. As I told you before, faith is a foundation that the soul dares venture upon. As that martyr said, "Though I cannot dispute for the truth, I can still die for the truth." Where faith comes with a convincing light, though there are doubts, fears, and temptations, yet it can trust and depend. The soul resolves, "If I perish, I will perish here. Let all the world say what they will, if I find this is the way, whatever comes of it, I will not go back." By this means, faith overpowers the soul and carries it through opposition. So faith is an evidence.

Many things should be said about application. First, if faith is an evidence to other things and makes them seen, then it is an evidence to itself. It is therefore possible for a soul to know its own good condition and its interest in Christ merely by the very work of faith itself. Though, for the present, it is not able to argue *aposteriori,* from the effects of faith, yet it may argue *apriori.* Faith may evidence itself. Many Christians go on in a doubting way merely because they think they must have evidences of their faith by some effects that follow faith. Until then they can have no comfort. It is true that where faith is, there will be fruits and effects of it, but if you could learn this mystery of the gospel, to find and evidence in faith itself, you would be comforted sooner. It is a great deal safer, too.

If you doubt your condition and fear your sins are not pardoned, if you fear you have no interest in Christ, the way to be freed from these fears and doubts is by renewing the act of faith itself, by presenting to your souls the riches of the grace of God in the Lord Jesus. See if viewing the glory of that will not draw out your soul to believe. And if upon this your hearts do not stir, set those things before your soul again. Do not turn from renewing the acts of faith to pore upon your corruptions, and then say that you can see no interest that you have in Christ. But look upward again and again, and, by the very viewing of them, a virtue will come in to draw the heart to believe.

By presenting the law, there is an efficacy to terrify and frighten, and by presenting the glorious things of the gospel there is an efficacy to draw out faith. Then you are to renew the very primitive work of faith, that is, to close with Christ and cast yourselves upon the freeness of the grace of God in Christ. And though you find such and such corruptions in your hearts and are ready to say, "Shall such a one as I, polluted and defiled, cast myself upon the grace of God in Christ?", yet lay hold upon Christ, and you have as much reason to do it from this as from anything. Therefore, this must be your course: to renew this primitive act of faith again and again.

You might say, "Aye, but my doubts and fears still remain." But if you would have evidence, do it again and again a thousand times over and at last there will be an evidence of the act of faith itself.

But you might say, "This may be presumption to cast oneself on the free grace of God in Christ." To this I answer that this is not presumption, because the very act itself gives you a right to all that is in God and Christ. Presumption is when a man takes that to which he has no right, and if a man does that which he has no right to do (but if that which he does gives him a right to do it), it is not presumption.

But you will say, "This is licentiousness and gives liberty to sin." Oh, do not wrong faith. When you, in the lack of sight and sense, can venture yourself upon the riches of the grace of God in Christ, though you can see no reason for it, it is the most glorious work that you can possibly do in this world. If you should live to overcome all your corruptions and to do the greatest service imaginable, it could not be as glorious a work as this.

It is the most difficult thing in the world, and therefore is not a doctrine of liberty to sin. The soul that can go through all the difficulties of faith, that can overcome its guilt, the terrors of the law, and, notwithstanding all that comes between God and itself, can still venture upon the free grace of God in Christ, may overcome all the difficulties of the world. Though we are in the dark and our sight and our sense and all else is gone, we must still exercise faith. If you would study to magnify God as a Christian, this is the only way.

There is a notable example of credit that Alexander gave to his physician, an example of the trust that he put in him in front of all his noblemen. Alexander was sick and someone advised him in a letter to take heed of his physician, Philip, for someone had paid him to poison Alexander. The physician brought him the poison and Alexander gave him the letter and drank the poison, intimating that he would not believe what was reported of him. This was a mighty honor done to his physician. And so, when you have no evidence in yourself, when you have many temptations that speak ill of the free grace of God in Christ and that tell you that Christ has left you and forsaken you, and that it would never be thus and thus with you if Christ really intended any good to you, and when temptations are in their greatest intensity and speak the worst of Christ, if you will venture your soul upon Christ, He will take it as the greatest honor you are capable of doing to Him. It is the readiest way to advance the riches of His grace and mercy.

Be afraid of unbelief as well as of presumption. Be afraid lest you should not magnify the free grace of God in Christ, which is His great design among the children of men. I wanted to lay down something to show what encouragement we have to believe in case of lack of evidence, when we are in the dark and can see no light, and to give rules to help our faith, but I will conclude with this one use.

By what has been delivered, you may see what an excellent and admirable grace faith is and of what use it is. Oh, brethren, in these times where there is such fear, trouble, and distraction, to have faith give a subsistence to all the things that God has spoken, a subsistence to all the glorious promises that God has made to His people, what a wonderful blessing this is! Exercise faith, and by faith give a subsistence to all these promises. Make them a foundation to rest upon. Be willing to venture all you have, your estates, names, liberties, and lives for the furthering and fulfilling of those glorious promises which God has made unto His church. If you have the kind of faith that gives foundations to those promises, you will do so.

Though we see nothing but darkness and misery in the world, still let us exercise faith. If the hour of temptation is yet to come, then we will need faith, and faith alone in such darkness can help us to light. To prepare for such times, labor to strengthen faith and, by what you have heard, you can see in what stead faith will stand you in any danger. It is a great comfort to a Christian that, though he is in the dark in many things (as there are many truths now disputed about churches and the like), yet he knows that he has that in him which will make the things of eternal life evident to him.

It is a wonderful blessing of God to have a principle that gives subsistence and evidence to such things as these are. How exceedingly would many poor souls rejoice if they might have an evidence of just one truth of religion, like the truth of a Deity which reason gives light in. They are so pestered with atheism that they would give a thousand worlds to be rid of it. Now if this is so great a mercy, to have that which evidences only one principle of religion, what a glorious mercy is it, then, to have faith to evidence all the glorious things of God and to make them plain and clear to you!

You can remember a time when you thought of them as fancies and conceits, but now you see them as clear as the light of the sun, and you would not see them any differently for a thousand worlds. Hereafter, brethren, when we shall see them not by faith, but by sense, oh, how shall we then bless God that we had evidence of these things made to our souls. What would have become of us if we had not had an evidence to clear those things to us that lead to this glory, to evidence the righteousness of God in Christ for eternal life. I saw these things subsisting and evident before, and now God reveals them fully to me. Whereas, on the other side, those that lack a principle of faith to make them substantial and evident to them, what a horrid terror it will be to them when they shall come to be substantial and evident to them! Then you will say, "O Lord, if I had seen these things before, my heart would never have been so taken with the things of the world. I ran madly after the vanities of the world, to get riches and honor, and I thought I was the only happy man and that those things were only substantial and real things. Those things I heard the preacher speak of I thought were only notions and conceits. But now I see that they are real and substantial. O, miserable man that I now am!"

O, the work of faith that can make those that are of weak parts to see the great things of God! James 2:5 says, *Hearken my brethren, God hath chosen the poor of this world to be rich in faith.* To understand the great things of faith, that poor men should understand the great, the deep, the glorious things of God that were hidden from the foundations of the world, is a wonderful work. Therefore, when John sent to Christ to know if He was the Messiah, Christ gave this as an argument, *the poor receive the gospel,* Matt. 11:5. Why was that an argument that Christ was the Messiah? Was it not rather an argument against Him that the poor did it? If the great ones had done it, it would have been an argument. No, the poor receive the gospel. And that those who are poor and weak in other things should have this mighty work wrought in their souls, to be able to receive Christ and the gospel, is an argument of the mighty power of God.

Brethren, to have the use of the eye of the body by which we can see the great works of God like the sun, moon, and stars, and by which we can take notice of the glory of God in these, is a great blessing. What man would be willing to lose his sight to gain a world? It reveals so much of the glory of God. Now if the eye that receives only these natural things is so precious, then what is it to have a principle within us, an eye of faith, clearly to evidence the great things and glorious counsels of God to us?

If a crystal that can receive colors into it from without is precious, what is the crystal of faith? It may well be called precious faith, for it receives into the soul the glory of God, the excellencies of Christ, and the great things of eternal life. These are brought into the soul by faith, in the reality and power of them to raise the heart and to fill it with all joy and peace in believing, to carry the soul through all the troubles of this world. Oh, the eye of faith is a precious eye! The eye of sense is precious because we can see visible objects by it, but the eye of reason is more precious because that can make things seen which are not seen by the eye of sense. Reason can discourse up to God Himself, and it is the wonderful excellency of a reasonable creature that God has given him that ability so that he can reason from the effect to the cause and from one cause to another until at last he gets up to God, the First Being of all.

This is an admirable endowment that we should bless God for. But now, if the use of reason has such an excellency in it, because by it we have an evidence of reasonable things to us, then go still higher and labor to have a right esteem of this precious faith that gives to us such evidence of the glorious things of God. This is that faith which God puts into our hearts on purpose, that by it we might be able to receive into our souls those glorious mysteries of godliness that infinitely concern our eternal peace.

This sermon was preached April 25, 1641.

SERMON 4
*"If the Son therefore shall make you free,
ye shall be free indeed."*
(John 8:36)

In this chapter we have Christ continuing His contest with the wrangling, peevish Jews, answering all that they said in spite of the fact that they snarled at nearly every word that passed. However it was with the multitude, though, there were still some who were taken with what He said, for in verse 30 it is said, *As He spake these words many believed on Him.* At least there were some beginnings of faith, or some preparations for it, and Christ tells them, verse 31, that if they continued in His Word, then they were indeed His disciples. It is as if He should say, "It is not enough that you are stirred for the present and profess that you believe in Me. I will not take you for My disciples unless you continue in My Word." How often the flashes that are upon the hearts and consciences of men vanish and come to nothing! They continue not in the Word of Christ and therefore are not His disciples.

Christ tells them further that they must understand more concerning their condition than they then apprehended, *And ye shall know the truth, and the truth shall make you free,* v.32, as if He should say, "Though you have some confused apprehensions of things for the present, you know only a little of your condition. But if you will go on in the way God is beginning with you in stirring your consciences, if you will continue, you shall come to know more than you

117

now know. You shall know the truth, and the truth shall make you free." And then in verse 33 they say, *We are Abraham's seed, and were never in bondage to any man; how sayest Thou, ye shall be made free?*

See here, they begin to snarl again. Master Calvin, I remember, thinks that these are the words of some other Jews that were present, not those who are said to believe. But others think it may be understood even of those that are said to believe for, though they began to assent to the doctrine of Christ and were very much convinced, there was still an abundance of frowardness, perverseness, and crookedness in their spirits. They began to wrangle with Christ, especially when He but intimates something to them about their bondage.

It is normal for many people who have some stirrings of conscience and some beginnings of the working of God's Spirit in them (and it may be saving ones, too) to continue a long time in their frowardness and perverseness of spirit if they are opposed in their way. Therefore they say, "Do you speak to us of bondage and tell us of freedom? Why, we were never in bondage to any!" (v.33) What! Never in bondage to any? Were not the Jews in bondage to the Babylonians when in captivity to them? Were they not at this very time in bondage to the Romans? And yet *we were never in bondage*.

Thus carnal hearts, until grace fully subdues them, are very loath to know their wretched condition. They love to not hear of anything that reveals to them the misery they are in. They were never in bondage, they say, yet Christ pities them. He did not take advantage of the opportunity to fling away because He saw them continuing still in their perverseness and snarling at what He spoke, but He tells them what bondage He meant. It is as if He should say, "The truth is, though you think yourselves free, there is still a bondage you are in, and such bondage that no one can deliver you from it but the Son of God alone. *If the Son therefore shall make you free, you shall be free indeed.*" Thus we come to the words of the text.

These words, then, hold forth the blessed liberty of the gospel to us, that freedom that believers have by Christ. I come, then, to the main doctrinal conclusion which is this: there is a blessed liberty that Christians enjoy by Christ and only by Him. This doctrine of Christian liberty that is enjoyed by Christ is a treasury of admirable consolation, and much of the mystery of the gospel is contained in this doctrine. I would enlarge my discourse too far, and seek to grip too much, should I think to give you even a view of this doctrine in all the points of it. If I were to handle it at large, I would have to show you (1) what it is that Christ sets believers free from; (2) the privileges of this freedom they have by Christ; (3) the subject of it, who it is that has this freedom; (4) by whom it comes, how it is by this Son and only by Him; (5) the price and purchase of this freedom; (6) the interest that believers have in this freedom, how they come to be enfranchised and to have interest in it; and (7) the application of it. But if I go to work this way, I would only be able to do a little. Therefore I will not grasp so much. I intend, therefore, to handle just one special thing in our freedom by Christ.

If I should show you what we are freed from, there is the freedom from the law, the freedom from the power of sin, the freedom from the bondage of fear, the freedom from an accusing conscience, the freedom from slavishness in the performance of holy duties (we are set at liberty in holy duties), the freedom from death and the evil of that, the freedom from the slavery of the devil, and the freedom from the ceremonial law. But neither must we seek to seize upon all these particulars. To show you our freedom in these, I shall only pitch upon one, and that is our freedom from the law. *If the Son therefore shall make you free, you shall be free indeed.*

This doctrine of freedom from the law is the subject that we are to handle at this time, and when I speak of freedom from the law I do not mean freedom from obedience to the law. It is an erroneous thought to think we are freed from obedience to the law. It is a fanciful idea too low and absurd for us to spend time on now since we have so little, and since we have to deal with a matter of such great consequence. What is the law but the image of God, the very beam of the wisdom and holiness of God Himself? For anyone to say that we should be freed from obedience to the law is as much as if they said that we should be freed from the image of God, from the beam of the wisdom and holiness of God Himself. Therefore, we will spend no more time on that, but when I speak of freedom from the law, I mean freedom from the rigor of the law, from the condemning sentence of the law in which all the rigor of it appears.

Wherefore, then, it is necessary to give you a view of the bondage that we are all in under the law, unless we are delivered by Christ. And then secondly, I shall endeavor to open to you in what the liberty of the gospel consists that Christ has purchased for us. These two things, brethren, have in them the chief doctrine of divinity and, unless you are well instructed and settled in these two, you cannot know any point of doctrine correctly.

I will be brief in the first point, though there are many particulars in it, for it is the second point I chiefly intend to deal with. To prepare for the first, I will tell you beforehand that I shall name many things to you that will seem exceedingly hard. But take this consideration along, that though the things I name to you appear never so hard, they are still in order to that which I shall afterward deliver to you that shall have this much comfort and peace in it. If I tell you anything of your bondage, it is only to this end: that you may know the blessedness of your freedom and liberty.

Wherefore, then, for the rigor of the law (that you may know what you are free from), you must know what this is and what you are all under by nature when you are out of Christ, for that is how the Holy Ghost expresses our subjection to the law. He says we are not under it, Romans 6:14, *Now ye are not under the law.*

There was a time when we were under the law. First, then, the rigor of the law is this: it requires hard things of those that were under it. I shall show you later how the things are not so to those that are set free by Christ, but to those who are under the law, it is a hard yoke. It requires hard things, things that are cross and contrary to the hearts and dispositions of all who are under it, things between which and their hearts there is enmity and antipathy. Now to require such things as one has no mind to, but are quite contrary to one's nature and that one's nature has an antipathy to, is very tedious. Yet such are all the duties of the law to those who are in bondage to it.

Secondly, the law requires not only hard, but impossible things, impossible to perform by those that are under it. The law is a yoke that neither we nor our fathers were able to bear, Acts 15:10. You may object that it is speaking of the ceremonial law, aye, but there is more in it, for just consider the occasion of that speech. It was upon this ground: that there were some that came from the church of Jerusalem to the church of Antioch. There they troubled the disciples with two doctrines, the doctrine of the necessity of the ceremonial law and the doctrine of being justified by the law. Now this church of Antioch wrote to the church at Jerusalem to be satisfied about both these questions, and that which is spoken about them both. It was not only the ceremonial law they were looking to for justification, but the moral law, too. Both were a yoke that neither they nor their fathers were able to bear. It must also mean both because in the very next words we find it opposed to the grace of Christ. In verse 11, *But we believe that through the grace of the Lord Jesus Christ, we shall be saved even as they.* It is as if he should say, "You must not think to be saved by the law, but by the grace of the Lord Jesus Christ."

Now the grace of the Lord Jesus Christ is opposed to our justification by obedience to the moral law as well as to the ceremonial, so that the moral law is a yoke that neither we nor our fathers were able to bear. It requires of us such things as are impossible to be done by those that are under it. We must not dispute now how this can be or the justice of it. That will come later.

Thirdly, the law exacts all of us under the condition of perfection. The law accepts nothing but that which is complete and absolutely perfect in every way, both in regard to the principle from whence, the manner how, the rule by which, and the end to which it requires absolute perfection.

Fourthly, the law accepts no surety. It must have it done in our own persons. It is like a severe creditor who will be paid the utmost farthing, and only by us. I say the law, in itself considered, looks for a perfect righteousness of our own or else it condemns us. This is the righteousness of the law, Rom.10:5, *That he that doth the things therein contained, shall live by them.* He that <u>does</u>; there must be doing, and that by himself personally or not at all.

But it may be that, though there is much required,

upon some endeavors there may be remission. In the fifth place, therefore, such is the rigor and severity of the law that, let us endeavor never so much to obey it, all our endeavors are rejected if they do not come up to perfect obedience. It is a vain plea of many people to say that they do what they can, they desire well and endeavor well. It is true, this is something to those who are children and have freedom by Christ but, to those who are under the law, endeavors to obey, though never so strong, are not accepted by God if the work is not done.

Sixthly, the law requires constancy in all these. Suppose we could obey the law or go very far in many things. Yet such are the terms between God and us (as we are under the law) that if we were able to obey the law in everything as long as we live until the very last moment, and should offend only in one particular at the very last moment, were it not for this freedom we have by the Son we would be utterly undone forever. You may see as you go of what infinite concern is our freedom in Christ. You must look to yourselves how you get deliverance by Christ, for certainly this is your condition as long as you are under the law.

Seventhly, the law exacts the obedience it requires in a violent way upon all that are under it. It comes as roughly upon them as Pharaoh's taskmasters. It requires the work and does not look at the strength. Strength or no strength, the work is required with dreadful threatenings if it is not performed. Therefore, it is the law that was delivered in such a dreadful manner with thundering, lightning, earthquakes and fire so that it made even Moses to shake and tremble at the manner of delivering it. In Deut.33:2 it is called a fiery law, it came with mighty rigor.

Eighthly, there is this rigor in the law, too, that upon any breach of the least thing it breaks the soul by its severity. It utterly disenables it to ever perform any obedience again. There is such a hardness in the covenant of the law. The law is like an iron or brass wall that, upon any breach of it the soul, is as an earthen vessel that dashes against it and is broken in pieces. There must be a creating power to make it whole again.

Consider, I beseech you, this is the condition of the covenant of works which was made with us in Adam (which is now the covenant of the law) that, upon any one breach, it breaks the soul by its severity so that it utterly disenables it to keep it again. It roots out all the principles whereby the soul should be enabled to obey again. Sins against the gospel do not do so, as you shall hear later. And this is the very ground why, upon the very first sin of Adam, all were gone. So were the angels upon their sin, because they had to deal with God only in a covenant of works. But if, upon the breach of the law, we come to have all principles rooted out by which we should keep it, later (we hope) it will pity us and not exact obedience.

Therefore, in the ninth place, notwithstanding this, the law goes on in its curse and requires as perfect an obedience to every part of it as if we had all the principles that might enable us to keep it still, and that upon

pain of eternal death. This is the severity of the law-
it does not at all remit the threatening, punishment, or
exactness of obedience, notwithstanding the fact that
we have lost all power to obey it.

In the tenth place, it requires this of us, but gives us
no strength at all to do what it requires. It finds us di-
vested of those principles that we once had to yield
obedience, and it affords us no new principles. Therefore, some have compared the severity of it to Pharaoh's taskmasters. It requires the tale of brick but
gives no strength at all.

In the eleventh place, it strikes at our life in all that
it does. The law is satisfied with no affliction. Let it
be transgressed in the least degree, all the afflictions
that can possibly be in the world will not satisfy it.
Such is the severity of it that it strikes at life and at
eternal life. It follows us to pursue us to our blood, to
temporal and eternal death. And here I might open the
condemning sentence of the law, but that would require
a subject by itself. Therefore I only name what is in
this heading, that it strikes at our lives upon every
transgression of it.

Twelfth, the severity of it is in this: that upon any
breach it binds the soul to eternal death by the stron-
gest bonds that possibly can be, though it does not execute it immediately. It suspends execution, but the
bond is immediately sealed upon the breach of it, so
that all men, upon every breach of it, have chains
clapped upon their souls, which is the guilt of sin
whereby they stand bound to eternal death by such

bounds as all created power in heaven and earth is unable to loose.

In the next place, such is the severity of the law that when once it is offended, amends can never be made by anything we are able to do. Suppose we have offended the law in some one thing, and that only once. If after this we should endeavor to do what we can for our lives and swelter our heart's blood to obey the law, and think to make up the breach we have made, yet we can never make amends again. It is true that some, though they are offended, may be pleased again by double diligence, but we must never think to do so with God. Being under the law, when we have broken it once, we cannot make amends with all our care and diligence. That is a great part of the severity of the law.

Aye, but what do we have to do except to mourn and cry and rent our hearts because of this distressed condition we are in?

Fourteenth, the law accepts no repentance. It will not discharge the guilt of any one sin for all the sorrow in the world. And here lies a great mistake of people: when they have offended they think they will be careful to make amends, and they will mourn and repent, etc. It is true, if you are under the covenant of grace this is something, but if you are in your natural condition, you can weep your eyes out and send streams of blood from your eyes in mourning for just one sin, a sin in thought, that which you count as a little matter. Should you resolve to cry out and mourn for that sin all your life, it will not be accepted unless you come under the blessed liberty purchased by Christ. Therefore, know the difference of being under the law and under the gospel.

Fifteenth, such is the rigor of the law that, when it has opened our wounds and miseries, it goes no further, it shows no means of deliverance. It is like a surgeon who opens the wound but applies no remedy. Certainly, were it not for a Mediator, we would find the law only to open our wound and there leave us.

Sixteenth, such is our bondage to the law that, instead of mortifying any of our sins, it rather stirs them up and makes them more. It threatens grievous things against its transgressors, but it does not mortify sin. It stirs up lust, though accidentally, and makes our sin sinful beyond measure.

Seventeenth, there is one more thing after all this. If we should keep the law, its promises are mean and low in comparison to the promises of the gospel. I do not say they are just temporal, though before the gospel was revealed there was only a little of spiritual promises, yet we know what the Apostle says, II Tim. 1:10, *That life and immortality is brought to light through the gospel.* And though I do not say there are none, yet there are very few Old Testament scriptures that speak of eternal life.

Thus you see your bondage under the law, and surely you will now think it a blessed condition to be freed from the law. It is one argument that a soul is delivered from the bondage of the law when it can hear all this and yield to God's justice in it and can have the heart raised to God in hearing it. But if the soul, upon hearing these things, thinks them so hard and unreasonable that it is ready to rise against them, it is a sign that the spirit is not acquainted with them. And although these things may seem hard to us, if we consider just three or four particulars they will not seem so hard.

First, consider that you have to deal with a God of infinite justice and worth. Indeed, if we look on God as we look upon a creature like ourselves, we would think it mighty hard, but now, when we have to deal with a God of infinite worth, we should not think it hard.

Second, we shall not think it hard if we consider that state of perfection in which God made man at first. However it is with us now, God did at first give us a stock to trade in the way of obedience, and to enable us to do what the law required.

Third, if you rightly understood what sin is, you would not think it hard that, upon sin, we should be given up to such a woeful condition as we have spoken of. If you look upon sin as that which strikes at an infinite Deity, at the very being of God Himself as much as in us lies, then you will not wonder that one sin should bring us into such a hard condition.

Fourth, if we consider those things that we all take for granted that are as hard as these, and lay them next to each other, they will not seem so hard. God cast the angels into eternal torments and did not even parley with them about any terms of peace. God, for one sin in Adam, condemned all mankind. You all grant this in general. God the Father dealt with His own Son, the Son of His love, in such a way that He made Him a curse for man and laid the weight of His wrath upon Him so as to make Him sweat drops of blood and cry out, *My God, My God, why hast Thou forsaken Me?* If you never heard of such a thing, this would seem as hard as anything we have spoken of.

Now before we come to speak of the other, let that which has been said teach that surely, then, all men in their natural condition are in a hard case. It is with them as it was with the Israelites when the bondage they were in under Pharaoh increased. The text says that they saw themselves in an evil case. Oh, that upon hearing these things, you would learn to see what you are out of Christ, that you would see yourselves in an evil case, in a sad and dangerous condition.

Secondly, if this is the case, that every soul is naturally under such a bondage to the law, then the saving of a soul is a great and mighty work, yea, such a work that God must move heaven and earth to save a soul and deliver it from the bondage of sin. The reason why people so slight this great work of salvation and mediation by Christ is because they do not know their bondage. Understand this bondage rightly, what it is to be under the law (I have not told you of the condemnation or the curse of the law, I have only set out to you the bondage of the law), and you will see by this that it is a great work to save a soul.

Thirdly, you may see by this how that vain plea of

carnal hearts comes to nothing. What will you trust now to your good meanings, good desires, and good intentions? You will mourn and grieve because yours are no better. You will do what you can for God. It is true these are good things, but are these the things you rest in for standing before God? If they are, certainly you do not know the terms you stand in to God or what your bondage is.

Fourthly, if God reveals Himself to a man only by the law, it is impossible but that the soul must fly from Him and look upon God and His law as enemies unless it is revealed together with the gospel. That is what I am now to tell you, that liberty we have by the gospel.

The liberty of the gospel is a precious liberty wherein the treasury of the mystery of grace is laid up. It is the only ground of support to our souls and St. Paul, who was the great instrument of God in opening the doctrine of the liberty of the gospel, sets it down in all his epistles, and in many places elegantly. One text which contains some difficulty is Galatians 4, from verse 21 on:

> *Tell me, ye that desire to be under the law, do ye not hear the law? For it is written, that Abraham had two sons, the one by a bond-maid, the other by a free woman: but he who was of the bond-woman was born after the flesh, but he of the free woman was by promise: which things are an allegory; for these are the*

two covenants, the one from the Mount Sinai, which gendereth to bondage which is Agar; for this Agar is Mount Sinai in Arabia, and answereth to Jerusalem which now is, and is in bondage with her children: but Jerusalem which is above, is free, which is the mother of us all: for it is written, rejoice thou barren that bearest not, break forth and cry thou that travailest not: for the desolate hath many more children than she which hath an husband.

The text seems to be somewhat obscure, and yet most excellently sets out this doctrine I am now on of bondage under the law and liberty under the gospel. The allegory, you see, is from the two sons. Abraham had one son by a bondmaid, another by a free woman. It is an allegory, says the Apostle, and it signifies the two covenants, the covenant of works and the covenant of grace. The covenant of works was from Mount Sinai. There the law was revealed, which is Agar, *for this Agar is Mount Sinai in Arabia.* I remember Luther says that Agar, in the Arabian tongue, is as much as Mount Sinai. They call it so in the Arabian tongue and so the Apostle alludes to it. Therefore, the law that is of Agar tends only to bondage. Agar's posterity were Gentiles and were in bondage, and were not to have the privilege of the sons of the free woman. Therefore, all those who have to deal with God in the covenant of works are bondmen and are not to have the privilege of the children of the free woman, of the children of God.

Well, *this Agar is Mount Sinai in Arabia, and answereth to Jerusalem, which now is, and is in bondage with her children.* He sets out the state of the church of the Jews, the Jerusalem that now is, to be in a state of bondage compared to the church of the gospel because they had so little knowledge of the gospel. They were in bondage to the law and knew little else but the law, but Jerusalem, which is above, is the state of the church under the New Testament. It is above in regard to the gospel, which is free and is the mother of us all. The church of God under the gospel is the Jerusalem which is above, *but now it is written, rejoice thou barren that bearest not, break forth and cry out thou that travailest not; for the desolate hath many more children than she which hath an husband.* That is, those who acknowledge the doctrine of the liberty of the gospel at first are just as desolate as the barren woman before it is revealed. Sarah was barren for awhile but later had a child, and so the doctrine of the liberty of the gospel is just a barren thing for awhile until people are acquainted with it.

We who are ministers of the gospel, it is our work to beget children to Christ. If we are legal and only preach the law, we would beget people to bondage, to Agar, but this is our chief work: to beget children to the free woman, to beget children to the free grace of God in Christ, and, oh, that there may be many here that are children of Agar, who may have had terrors and fears in their consciences and are still just children of the bond-woman! It is the gospel that proclaims the trumpet of jubilee to those that are under bondage. Therefore, it is observable at what time the trumpet of jubilee was to be blown, Lev.29:9, *Then shalt thou cause the trumpet of jubilee to sound, on the tenth day of the seventh month, in the day of atonement shall ye make the trumpet sound throughout all your land.*

What was this day of atonement? It was the day of public humiliation for all the people for their sins. The day of fasting and prayer appointed by God to afflict their souls is called a day of atonement, and the trumpet to proclaim the jubilee must be blown upon that very day wherein the people had been afflicting their souls for their sins. Therefore, now, if there is any soul that has been humbled before the Lord and has been afflicted for sin, behold, this is the work that is now to be done: blow the trumpet of jubilee to such a soul, proclaim liberty in the name of Christ to him and, as the Psalmist says, Ps.89:15, *Blessed is the people that know the joyful sound.* It is translated by some, "They are blessed that know the sound of the jubilee." This jubilee having reference to our jubilee by Christ, blessed are they that hear this joyful sound that we have here in the gospel.

Now the first joyful sound of the jubilee and liberty we have proclaimed by Christ from the law is this: your eternal state shall not be determined by the law. The law may terrify you, but it shall not determine your eternal state. It must do that for the children that are in bondage to it, but if you are a believer in Christ, if you are a child of the free woman, this is your liberty: the law shall not determine your eternal state. We do not love to have any business of great concern determined by those that are rigid and severe, so be of good comfort, oh believer. You have heard of much severity in the law, but the great business concerning your soul and eternal estate is above the law. It has nothing to do with you. You hear, many times, dreadful threats of the law, and these threats may often terrify you. You may be ready to say, "Who can stand before this holy God?" But peace be to you, you believing soul, for you are set at liberty from the law by Christ, and this is the first joyful sound.

The second joyful sound of liberty you have by the gospel is this: your Lawgiver is none other than He who is your Husband. You have to deal with none other, now, in the matters of your soul, but with Him who is your Husband and your Advocate, by whom all is ruled. I John 1:21 says, *If we sin, we have an advocate with the Father.* That is, you now have to deal with Christ your Lawgiver who, upon every transgression, is your Advocate with the Father, who stands up to plead for you and to answer all accusations against you. He that undertakes for you and engages all the interest He has in His Father for you is the One with whom you have to deal regarding your soul and eternal estate. This is the second joyful sound you have of the trumpet of the jubilee of the gospel, of the liberty you have by Christ.

Thirdly, being delivered from the bondage of the law, this is now your liberty, that you are now made a law to yourself. I mean this: there is nothing now required of you that is not written on your heart. God writes His law on tablets of stone, and all that is required of you in obedience to it is written on your heart. So that you do not now yield obedience to the law because of the condemning power of it and punishment due unto it as you do from a principle of love to it. We must know that we are not set free by Christ <u>from</u> obedience to the law. We are bound to obey the law still, but here is the difference: we are not servile to the law. We keep it freely. You keep the law now by being a law unto yourself and having all that God requires of you in His law written in your heart by the law of sanctity He has given you. This is the third joyful sound.

The fourth joyful sound is this: by the liberty you now have in Christ, this is your condition. Whatever you do, though there are never so many imperfections in it, if God can spy out the least good thing in you, He will take notice of that and cast away all evil. If God sees anything of His own Spirit in you He will be sure to take notice of that. If there is just one dust of gold, though it is mixed with an abundance of dross, God will not lose it but will find it. God is not strict to mark what is done amiss by His children, but He is strict to mark what is done well by them. Indeed, the law tells us, nay, a moral man will tell us, that to make an action good all circumstances must concur. But the liberty of the gospel tells us that where there is any good, any grace in action, God observes and takes notice of that.

To give an instance of this, and it is an excellent one for this purpose, in I Peter 1:3-6, the Apostle propounds Sarah as a pattern for good women, *Even as Sarah obeyed Abraham, calling him Lord.* She never called him Lord except when she did it unbelievingly, but God takes notice of that word and never mentions her unbelief. Now Sarah was a free woman and this is the gracious dealing of God with the free woman. If you are a child of the free woman, this is your privilege: that God will take notice of every good action that you do, Is.42:3, *A bruised reed shall He not break, and the smoking flax shall He not quench.* The word signifies that as soon as the flax begins to be black, God will not reject it. So that if there is the least degree of good, it is accepted, and that is the fourth joyful sound.

The fifth joyful sound is this: suppose you cannot do anything. If there is even a will, a desire in you, God accepts the will for the deed. Many carnal hearts please themselves with this, but this is the case of those that are set at liberty by Christ. Perhaps you cannot pray, but present yourself before God as the Apostle says and that shall be accepted by God. Know this, that if there is any excuse to be made for you, Christ will find it and make it before God for you. That is the fifth joyful sound.

The sixth thing in which the liberty we have by Christ consists is that, though the gospel calls for obedience, it does it in such a sweet and loving way that it would make any heart in the world fall in love with it. It draws by the cords of love. II Cor.5:20 says, *Now then we are ambassadors for Christ, as though Christ did beseech you by us: we pray you in Christ's stead, be ye reconciled to God.* And Phil.2:1 says, *If there be therefore any consolation of Christ, if any comfort of love, if any fellowship of the spirit, if any bowels and mercies, fulfill ye my joy, etc.* The gospel does not come as the law upon Mount Sinai with thunder, lightning, and darkness, but it comes in a mild and gentle way, and by that allures and draws the soul unto itself. And that is the sixth joyful sound.

The seventh joyful sound of the gospel is that the gospel and the liberty of it comes gently with an abundance of life and strength. It comes as the Spirit is, and where the Spirit is there is power, as the Apostle says. I remember Luther had this note on Romans 8. He said that the law is a spiritual law because it is the law of God, but it is not the law of the spirit of life. It is the law of the gospel that brings the spirit of power and life along with it. A virtue goes together with the demands of the gospel to strengthen the soul to obedience, and the gospel gives grace and strength beyond what Adam had in two ways. The grace that Adam had was only a power to do, but the will and the deed were not given. The grace of the gospel, though, gives the power, the will, and the deed.

The eighth joyful sound is that tender pity and compassion that is in God to those that are made free by it. This is the difference between the sins of those that are under the law and those under the gospel: the sins of those under the law make them hated by God, but the sins of those under the gospel make them pitied by God.

The ninth joyful sound is this: the gospel has a mighty efficacy to melt the heart and to resolve it into sorrow and mourning, such mourning that is one of the most acceptable things in the world to God. The law, I told you, does not accept repentance, but the gospel does. The tears of repentance that come from believers, next to the blood of Jesus Christ, are the most precious things in the world. I say this, next to the drops of the blood of Christ, the drops of your tears, coming from evangelical repentance, are most acceptable to God. This is the ninth joyful sound.

Tenth, another is this: the gospel comes with healing. As it has a melting power, so it has a healing power. Christ is described as coming with healing in His wings. Water makes the lime burn more, but oil, which provokes other things to burn, quenches that. So it is with the oil of the gospel. Christ was anointed for this purpose: to heal you and to quench your lusts and corruptions. In Is.57:18 we have an excellent promise. Verse 17 says, *He went on frowardly in the way of his heart.* Now mark what follows, *I have seen his ways, and I will heal him.*

The eleventh joyful sound is that now being set at liberty by Christ, though you sin not only against the law but against the gospel, your sins against the gospel shall not have power to root out any habits of grace, but the grace of the gospel will still uphold the habits of grace in your soul. It is otherwise with the law, for one offense against the law not only roots out the habit that is contrary to the offense, but all other habits also. The grace of the gospel, though, is such that the habits of grace within us are not touched.

The twelfth joyful sound is this: the gospel is so full of grace that it takes advantage of our misery. This is a good argument of the tenor of the gospel, *Pardon my sin, O Lord, for it is great.* Strange argument of the child of the bond-woman, but a good argument of a child of the free woman, and it is God's argument, Gen.8:21, *I will not destroy the world again, for the imagination of man's heart is evil from his youth.*

Thirteenth, another joyful sound of the gospel is this: the gospel proclaims liberty to us that all that is required of us may be done, accepted by, and from another, Jesus Christ.

Fourteenth, the grace of the gospel shows wherein God shall have all the wrong done to Him by your sins made up. Suppose the gospel had proclaimed that God was willing to pardon. This would not be enough as long as God stood wronged. But now the gospel not only proclaims to you that God is content to forgive all your sins, but it tells you of a way how that God shall have all the wrong that you have done to Him made up. His Son, who has set you at liberty, has undertaken it and has done it.

Fifteenth, another joyful sound of the gospel is

this: that there is a most absolute, perfect righteousness made over to us. The righteousness of the Son of God is yours, made over to you, to be presented before the Father for you.

Sixteenth, there is this joyful sound of the gospel. It proclaims admirable promises, glorious and high things, even the infinite treasures of God's grace. The Son is come from the bosom of the Father and has opened the treasures of the grace of God, and has revealed those things which were kept secret from the foundations of the world.

Seventeenth, there is still one more thing that is necessary for the full consolation of the liberty of the gospel and this blessed jubilee, that it may make a jubilee indeed in your heart, and that is this: such is the covenant of the gospel, and Christ has so undertaken it for you, that it shall never be forfeited. This is the full, rich, and glorious grace of the gospel, that now Christ has undertaken and engaged Himself to the Father, and the Father has promised and engaged His own truth, mercy, and faithfulness that this covenant shall never be forfeited. Yea, the very condition of the covenant that is required of you is that which Christ has undertaken to the Father to perform in you. If persevering is a spiritual blessing, it is part of the purchase of Christ and must stand and, therefore, peace be unto you. You are in such a condition that you cannot forfeit and break your covenant. The marriage covenant between you and your Savior can never be dissolved.

I should have shown you a little more of the blessedness of this liberty, that all this grace comes in and by the Son, not from the bounty of God in general but in a higher way. We are set at liberty by the Son of God, being made one with Him who is God and man, the Heir of all things, and so we are made co-heirs with Him, but I must break it off here.

"...but after this the judgment..."
(Hebrews 9:27, the latter end of the verse)

The scope of the Holy Ghost in this epistle is to prove the excellency of Christ, that He is the Messiah who was to come into the world, and that all the types and shadows of the law pointed to Him. A special part of this epistle is to show the excellency of the priesthood of Christ by preferring it above the priesthood of Aaron among other regards in this: that those priests offered up sacrifices often, but Christ offered Himself just once. This one time offering of Himself was available forever and needed no further offering. The Holy Ghost illustrates this by comparing the efficacy of Christ's sufferings with the efficacy of what a man does here in this world. The actions of men here in this world, whatever they are, whether good or evil, are available forever. What a man does in this life, accordingly, comes to be stated eternally when he dies. So the death of Christ is available forever, *It is appointed for men once to die and then comes judgment.*

By judgment, I do not think the Holy Ghost means the judgment of the great day (though it is true that, after death, the judgment of the great day will follow and all men must come to judgment, but I shall not speak one word of the judgment of that day), but there is another judgment that I think is intended by the Holy Ghost here, and that is the particular judgment that passes upon every soul immediately after death, which is the stating of the soul's eternal condition, either of happiness or misery.

While men live here, their condition is not stated by any act of God (though in regard of His eternal purpose, it is the same forever). Even the saints themselves would be in much hazard and danger about their everlasting state were it not that the grace of God is above them. The people of God in this life are not without fears and doubts about their everlasting condition, and what would many poor children of God give to be delivered from their fears and doubts, which are a grievous burden to them, that they might never have any more fear or doubt about their eternal states?

Well, if you are godly, in a little while it will be so with you. This is the good that death will bring unto you, that is, you shall be actually stated in your everlasting condition as to be beyond all hazard about it. You shall be beyond all fears, doubts, and temptations. You shall never fear again, never doubt again, never be tempted again, never again lose any of the good that you possess. This is the judgment that comes to the saints after death.

And, on the other side, wicked men here in this world are not without their hope and confidence that all shall be well with them, but after death comes judgment for them. That is, as we have it in Proverbs 11:7, when a wicked man dies, his hope perishes. He is sealed in such a condition as he is never likely to have hope of good again. He is past all hope and possibility of ever receiving further mercy from God, and this is the meaning of the text on both hands, that after death comes judgment. Whatever men's conditions are here in this world, though the saints have many fears and doubt about their estates, yet immediately after death they shall be sealed with and possessed of happiness, that they shall never doubt again. And even though wicked men in this world have many hopes and confidences and bless themselves in their way, immediately after death all shall vanish, for then judgment shall come. Job had this expression in Job 8:14, *The hope of the hypocrite is as the spider's web*. He spins out of his own spirit a cunning web, but the broom of death sweeps it all away, for immediately after death he comes to judgment.

This is the doctrinal conclusion we are to handle out of these words thus opened to you: the only time men have to provide for their eternal condition is the time of this life. If it is not done here, there is no help afterwards, for after death comes judgment. I shall desire to handle this point as far as it may be a ground to work upon your hearts and to stir you up in the time of your lives to make all sure between God and your souls, for after death comes judgment.

The point that I am now about to treat is one of the most serious things that concerns the children of men, and usually one of the first things that the Lord settles upon the hearts and consciences of those He converts to Himself. A man going in on his ways of sin and death can still think to himself, "Lord, where am I? What am I doing? What is likely to become of me? Why was I born? Why did I come into the world?

What have I to do here?" Then God answers, "That which you have to do here, and are sent into the world for, is to make provisions for eternity." It is about this great business, to make up all between God and your soul. So look to it that you are careful in it for, though your life is short and uncertain, this great business depends on this short and uncertain time of your life, and if it is neglected in this little space of time God gives to you, you are lost and undone forever. For after death comes judgment, and you shall then be sealed so that there can be no alteration.

It is the observation of schoolmen that what befell the angels that sinned, in death befalls wicked men. That is, as the angels, upon their first act of sin, were immediately sealed in an irrecoverable condition, so wicked men, when they die, are sealed in an irrecoverable condition. It is true that while we live in this world, though we are sinful, our condition is to be looked upon as better than the condition of the fallen angels. Here there is not an actual sealing of us, but, once death comes, a wicked man is then in that same condition with the devils themselves. That is, his condition is then so sealed and made certain and sure, and as irrecoverable as any of the angels that sinned. While we preach to men, though never so wicked and ungodly, because an actual judgment has not passed upon them, we are to offer grace and mercy to them in Christ, but if this offer is neglected for awhile, if the twine thread, the single thread of your life is once cut, then you are gone forever, for after this death comes judgment.

In the meditation of this point, I think I cannot help but look upon God as beholding all the children of men in their fallen, lost, sinful, and miserable estate with pity and compassion, saying, "Poor creatures, they have sinned against Me and have made themselves liable to eternal wrath, which they do not understand and which they are not able to bear. Well, I will grant them a little time to solicit a pardon and to come in and make their peace with Me, and I will give them the means for that end. But let them look to themselves, for according to the improvement of the time that I now give them, so shall it be with them to all eternity. If they neglect it, they are gone forever. Mercy shall do them no good."

The tenor upon which we all hold our lives is no other than that of a malefactor condemned to die who has a little time of reprieval granted to him through the favor of the prince, and some intimation given of a possibility in that time to solicit his pardon. According to how he spends that time, so shall it be with him for life or death. Thus I say that we all hold our lives. We are all condemned before the Lord, only God has, out of His infinite grace, provided a way and means of salvation for the children of men, and gives us a little time to look about us, to provide for the making of our peace with Him and, if that is neglected, all is gone and we are undone forever.

Great things, then, depend upon this uncertain, small time of our lives. It is reported of Alexander that, when he went against any city, he used to set up a burning lamp, and would make proclamation that whoever came in while this lamp was burning would find favor and have his life, but whoever stayed until that lamp went out was a dead man and must expect no mercy. Brethren, know that God has set up a lamp and proclaims, "Whoever comes in while this lamp is burning shall find mercy, but if you stay until the lamp is out, there is nothing but eternal misery to be expected." This lamp of your lives may not only go out upon the consumption of the oil, but it may be put out by accidental means. If this lamp is out once and your work is not done, you are undone forever.

We read in I Kings 6:7 that when Solomon was preparing the temple, he made all things ready beforehand so that there was no noise of axe or hammer heard there. Whoever God intends for a living stone in the glorious temple of heaven, He squares and fits them there. What is to be done must be done here, nothing will do it hereafter.

Whatever thou hast to do, do it with all thy might; for there is no work, nor device, nor knowledge, nor wisdom in the grave whither thou goest, Ecc.9:10. And chapter 11:3 says, *In the place where the tree falleth there it lieth.* Which way you fall when you die, that way you shall lie eternally. If God-ward, then God is yours forever. If sin-ward, then misery and destruction is yours forever. Ecc.12:7, *Then shall the dust return to the earth as it was, and the spirit shall return unto who gave it.* The souls of wicked men return to

God that gave them as well as the souls of the godly. That is, they return to God to receive the sentence of their eternal doom from Him and to be sealed in their everlasting condition. There is a mighty change in the soul immediately after it has departed from the body and is brought to stand before the glorious God to be sealed in its eternal condition.

There are twelve hours in the day wherewith a man may work, *but the night comes when no man can work*, says Christ in John 9:4. The time of this life is your working time, but the night is coming and then no man can work. We read in Revelation 6:8, *And I looked, and behold a pale horse, and his name that sat on him was death, and hell followed him.* Hell immediately follows death where death surprises any in their natural condition who have not finished the work of making their peace with God. II Cor.5:10 says, *We must all appear before the judgment seat of Christ, to receive according to what they have done in the flesh, whether it be good or bad.* It is not according to what we do afterwards, but according to what we have done here in the flesh. So it must be with us forever. There can be no repenting, no believing after this life. Body and soul being departed, the whole man is not capable of a work of God upon it.

And besides, immediately after death, God takes all means away. You shall never hear a sermon again, never have another admonition, never have good counsel again, never have any more working of God's Spirit to draw your souls to Christ.

And not only so, but God withdraws Himself so fully, in regard to the common works of His Spirit, that there is a kind of sealing the soul in sin (which cannot so properly in regard of God be said to be sin as evil) so that it shall be impossible for you to do anything but sin. Though while the saints live here they have many lusts and corruptions in them, immediately after death their souls are so fully possessed of the Spirit that they cannot sin. So on the contrary, while wicked men live here they have divers common gifts of God's Spirit and many restraints upon them, but immediately after death they are so fully separated from God, and God so fully withdraws Himself from them, that it is impossible for them to do anything else but sin and rebel against God and blaspheme Him to His face.

There was an innocency in Adam, a possibility to have not sinned. There is in us, while we are in this world, an impossibility that we should not sin. But in the world to come, there is an impossibility that the saints should ever sin. Look how the impossibility is on the other hand with the saints, so is the impossibility directly contrary on the other hand with the wicked. Therefore, the wicked must be sealed in an everlasting evil condition. There is no more possibility for the damned souls in hell to ever do anything but to blaspheme God than there is a possibility for the saints in heaven ever to sin against God.

Further, at the great day Christ gives up the kingdom to the Father, there will be another manner of administration than before. Christ will not be exercised in the work of His mediatorship, to mediate any further for those for whom He did not mediate in this life. After the separation of the soul from the body, the Spirit of God wholly departs from the soul, and the wrath of God is fully let out upon it so that it breaks the soul and fills up every faculty of it. It is impossible, in regard to the strong current of divine wrath that carries the soul along with it, that it should ever be exercised to all eternity any one moment in anything but the bearing of torment and divine wrath. As the saints shall be filled with the presence of God, and shall be carried on with such a strong current of divine mercy that it shall be impossible for their souls to be exercised in any other thing but the enjoyment of God and living to His praise, it is quite the contrary with the wicked. Therefore, after death, there is a sealing of both. I will enlarge myself no further in the opening of this point, but will come to apply it, for this point is applicatory rather than doctrinal. I shall content myself with three or four branches of application and then conclude.

In the first place, from this we can see what cause we have to bless God for the continuance of our lives, especially any that are here this day who have not thoroughly made their peace with God, who are not, upon certain and infallible terms, in this great business of providing for their eternal estates. If any doubts remain in your heart concerning your eternal condition, and if the fears of eternity have been upon your spirit, you will, from this point that has been spoken, see cause to bless God with your face upon the ground, adoring the riches of His grace that you are alive this day! Why? Because your life is the time of making up your peace with God. It is the time of providing for your eternal condition. If your life is at an end and this work is not done, then all is gone. Then judgment comes and you will be infallibly and unalterably sealed in a lost and undone condition. Therefore, it is well that you are alive this day.

If a man has a great business to do that concerns his whole life or estate, and it must be done in a very short time, what a favor he would count it to have his time lengthened even a little because his business is of great weight. He thinks to himself, "If I miscarry in it, I am lost and undone forever." So all those who have their lives here cannot help but sit down and bless God for lengthening their lives. The time of this life is a happy time. It is a day of grace, a day of salvation.

Oh, how happy would those poor creatures upon whom this judgment is passed, who are sealed in their eternal condition, think themselves if they might have just one day in which it might be said that there is a possibility for them to make provision for themselves concerning their eternal estate! As they were not long since, so you are now. And therefore, know how to prize your life. Oh, the lives of men and women (especially such as have not yet done that great work) are worth a thousand, thousand worlds. I remember hearing of a speech made by a great gentleman who was very sick, and his physicians told him there was no way for him but death. "Oh," he said, "that I might live, though it were just as a toad!" And indeed, what man or woman is there who does not have a thorough and Scripture assurance of this great work, that their peace is made with God, but who may, upon this very ground (if sickness is upon them), desire to live though only as a toad, because such great things depend upon their lives here in this world?

Brethren, say this to your own hearts upon serious meditation of that which I am now speaking. What if God should come now to this congregation and say to every one of you, "Well, now, the time that I have given you to provide for your eternal estate is at an end. If you have done your work, well and good. You shall be saved and shall possess eternal glory, but you must be cast according to that which is now done." I fear if such a message should come from heaven to many of us, it would make our hearts to ache within us and we would cry out, "O Lord, give me a little space before I go hence and am seen no more. Oh, that I might yet have a little more time!"

Suppose God had taken you away when He took away such a kinsman or kinswoman of yours, such a neighbor or friend, and death had come then and judgment had been passed upon you. Which way do you think you would have been cast? Cannot some of you remember that if God had taken you away at such a time, or when such a one died, you were then in such a case that you have reason to think you would certainly have been sealed in a condition of eternal misery? Therefore, bless God that you are alive this day to hear of such a doctrine as this, that as long as you live God gives you time to provide for your eternal estate.

Psalm 78:38 says, *God did not stir up all His anger, but called back His wrath.* When sickness comes upon men and women, some part of God's anger is let out. Aye, but if God had let out His anger just a little more, what would have become of you? You would have been gone, one stroke more would have cast you forever! Aye, but God was pleased to call back His anger and did not stir up His wrath. Oh, bless God for sparing you at such a time, for certainly, had you died then, your condition would have been as irrevocable as the devils themselves. Now is the day of grace. Now you have the voice of salvation sounding in your ears, but then you would have been past the time of grace, past praying, and past repentance. Now that you are not past this day, you are to prize your lives, and, brethren, know wherein consists the worth of your lives and the continuance of them.

There is a horrible impudence in some men. They would have their lives lengthened to have their lusts more satisfied. Did God give you your life for this end? No, the reason you should desire to live is that you may have more time to make provision for that which is of such infinite consequence, which, if not done, it would have been better for you to have been a toad, or a serpent, or the vilest creature that ever lived. Oh, that we had hearts to give God the glory of our lives and to prize our lives rightly. Excellent hearts would proceed from it were our hearts wrought to these things!

Secondly, if the only time we have to provide for eternity is the time of this life, how then are those to be reproved that misspend and squander away this precious time of their lives on vanities, and neglect the great business for which they were sent into the world? If such great things depend on our lives, then the loss of the time of our lives is a most dreadful loss. We all say that time is precious, and it is so, and the thorough understanding and applying of this point would make us see time as precious, indeed. If there could be an extract of the quintessence of all the pearls in the world put into one, it would not be such a precious pearl as the time of our lives, because that which depends on it is infinitely worth more than ten thousand worlds. However, men and women make little of their time. They play and sport it away. Yet there is no moment of your time that you misspend but you ought to know that it might be the very moment upon which your eternal condition depends.

You travel abroad and are merry and gay, and misspend your time and abuse yourself. I say, you ought to know that the instant of your sinning might be the very moment upon which the very hinge of all your eternal condition depends. If we understood this doctrine rightly, we would see it as an exceedingly great evil and folly to misspend our precious time. Men ordinarily live in the world as if they had nothing to do here but make provision for the flesh. If a man should come to the city on a business that concerned his life, and his time was very short, how industriously do you think he would spend that time? Every time the clock strikes it would strike his heart.

Suppose that God should send a damned soul from hell into the world again and should say thus to him, "Soul, you shall go and live again in the world, and I will give you a little space. You shall live a quarter or half a year, and I will put you in such an estate that there shall be a possibility for you to make your peace with me and to deliver yourself from this misery you are under." I appeal to you, how do you think such a one would spend his time? Now since you are persuaded in your consciences how such a one would spend his time, do you labor to spend your time in the same way?

Many would have rules to guide them in their way. Then take this rule: if such a thing could be, that a damned soul could be sent into the world again and be in a possibility of another estate, whatever you think such a one should do, that is what you should do. If one should come and say to him, "What can I give you for your time?" how he would condemn him! If you were to offer him crowns and kingdoms, yea, all the world for his time, he would scorn such an offer and prize one day more than a thousand worlds. Now you have had days and weeks, one after another, and yet you know you are liable to eternal ruin, and you do not know whether you have a week or a day more before your eternal condition is sealed upon you. Oh, what need do you have, then, to improve your time!

How few think of the passing away of their time, or that any great matter depends upon the time of their lives here in this world! You would count it a great folly and madness if a man had a precious oil that was worth a thousand pounds a pint and used it to light a lamp to talk or play or do trifling things by! A lamp that is fed by such oil is worth thousands! Surely this lamp should be for some weighty business, not for trifles. Know this, brethren, that the time of your lives is this lamp, lit up and fed with precious oil. Oh, do not squander it away, then, on trifles and vanities, for there are things of infinite concern that you have to do in this time of your lives. It is the great charge of Christ against Jezebel, Rev.2:21, *And I gave her space to repent of her fornication, but she repented not.*

I remember an expression of a woman who was in great distress of conscience. Some came to her and did what they could to persuade her that there was hope of mercy for her. But she looked at them with a ghastly countenance and said, "Call time again, call time again," as if she had said, "If you can, call time again, there may be hope for me."

Certainly we do not think of what depends upon time. It is a good sign of an enlightened conscience to make conscience of time. There is nothing that will put a more serious frame into a man's spirit than to know the worth of his time. Suppose that there was a company of men sailing to sea. They come at last to a little island that lies in the midst of the sea, many thousands of miles from any other land, and go and refresh themselves upon the island. But the captain warns them, "Look to yourselves, do not get far away. Be within my call, for I will not stay for any of you." The old men are afraid to go too far, but the young men trust their legs and think they can make haste. But the captain leaves and they are left behind and perish. It is true, while we are here in this world we are refreshing ourselves, but be sure, says God, that you are ready when I call. And God's call is the time of death. Now God calls and poor creatures are not ready, so they perish eternally. Oh, the loss of the time of your lives will be a dreadful loss one day, and it will pierce your souls to think that once you had a day of grace but now you have no more time. Judgment has been passed upon you and there is no remedy.

It is reported of a woman who had her house on fire that she was very busy and spent her time saving trifles, forgetting her child who was in the cradle. When she looked at what she had saved she saw a few trifling things, but then it came to her mind, "Oh, what has become of my child?" Imagining that her child had been burned (though it was saved), she ran mad to think that she had been so foolish as to mind things of no value and to forget her child. Take heed that it not be your case. You hear that time is precious and that there are some great things that concern your soul and eternal condition which you have to do. You spend your time to get estates, to get a little pleasure or honor in the world. But now, when the conclusion of all shall come, you shall look back to see what you have done, and God shall come and call you to an accounting saying, "Well, now is the end of your time, what have you done in the world?" Perhaps you can say, "Lord, I have gotten an estate and I have led a merry and jovial life." But all this time what have you done for eternity? What have you done about those things that are of such infinite weight and consequence?

Your heart will be overwhelmed with this thought, "O Lord, I forgot my soul. I had no thoughts about my eternal state. I have spent a great deal more time playing than praying, at least more time playing than praying to God in private to make my peace with Him." However it may be with you here, it will be a dreadful thing to you hereafter when you shall know what was the business of your time and what you were born for. I remember Bernard had a notable expression, speaking of some calling one to another, "Come, let us be merry until an hour has passed." He said, speaking with indignation against such folly, "What, will you do thus and thus until an hour has passed until time has passed? What, pass away that which the mercy of your Creator has so far indulged you as to give it to you for repentance and to get grace and to obtain pardon?" What, to pass away time in which you ought to be breathing after that life and blessedness which you have lost?

It becomes men who have not made their peace with God to spend their days bewailing their sinful and miserable condition, and not in merriment and frivolity, in chambering and wantonness. How you will one day wish that your time had been spent rather in mourning and lamenting! Abraham said to Dives, *Son, remember that in your lifetime you received your pleasures.* This life is not the life of your sensual pleasures, but to make all even between God and your soul. When God is so gracious as to give us space for great ends as He does in this world, He expects that all the children of men should spend their days seeking His face, making their peace with Him, prizing His mercy, and admiring and adoring the riches of His grace and goodness in His Son. But where do we find this? What a different course of life is there in most men from what God expects? They are guilty of desperate folly who squander away their precious time, seeing that it all depends on it.

Thirdly, if after death comes judgment, certainly, then, when death finds any man unprepared in a state of unregeneracy, who has not made his peace with God, it must be exceedingly dreadful because it brings judgment and seals such a one in his eternal condition. In Job 18:14, death is called the king of terrors, and well may it be so for, indeed, it is the most dreadful thing in the world to those that understand the meaning of their own sinful state and condition. There is enough in this to daunt the heart of the most profound, most stubborn wretch that lives on the earth, to consider that he is now launching into the ocean of eternity. God knows he has made little provision for it. "It may be it is the ocean of the wrath of this infinite God that I am now launching into," he says, "and must be in forever."

Certainly, unless you have a good assurance of the work done between God and your soul, the sight of the infinite ocean you are launching into immediately after death cannot help but make you give a dreadful shriek when you see that you are now likely to miscarry eternally. When death takes an ungodly man, it is nothing but cutting the thread upon which he hung over the pit of eternal misery. It is pulling up the flood gates of God's eternal wrath. Here, when afflictions are upon men and women, God's wrath is only like the little drops of water through the floodgates, but there is a vast difference between those drops and when the floodgates are pulled up. Then the streams gush out abundantly.

So it is with God's dealings with ungodly men here in this world. It may be that God's hand is upon them in many afflictions, but there are only a few drops of His wrath. But when death comes and finds them unprepared, then God pulls up the floodgates and the streams of the wrath of the Almighty overflow them. Death will be to them nothing more than the sergeant of the Lord of Hosts to take them to prison. It will be taking up the drawbridge. It will be a dismal and dreadful sunset that brings with it a night of eternal darkness, and that is a most dreadful sunset that shall never have day again.

Know that at death the day of grace and salvation sets for you, and an eternal night of dismal darkness will be upon you, so that when you are going out of this world and have not made your peace with God, then you must bid farewell to all comforts and whatever you enjoyed. Farewell to those excellent truths from the mouths of God's ministers again. Farewell to all my loving friends in whom I have rejoiced so much, and all the merry meetings that I have ever had. I shall never have them again. Farewell now, wife, husband, children, I shall never see your faces again. Yea, farewell to house and lands and all delights. Farewell to the sun, moon, and stars, and all the world. I shall never see you again until I see you at the great and dreadful day of Christ. And now I am leaving the world and all the comforts here, and all the means of grace here, and O Lord, where am I going?

It was a speech of Pope Adrian when he was about to die, "Oh, my soul, my soul, where are you going? You shall never be merry again as you wanted to be." It is a grievous thing for a poor creature whose time has come not to know where he is going, to think of former pleasures and delights, and never to have them again. When I consider the death of any ungodly man, Isaiah 10:3 comes to mind, *And what will you do in the day of visitation?* It is true, you now shuffle through the world, and take your fill of pleasure, and bear all before you. You have your mind set, and are stout and stubborn in your ways, and scorn the truth of God by His ministers, but what will you do in the day of visitation when the time shall come that puts an end to your days here?

Oh, the change that will be in your spirit then! God

will look upon you then with indignation and say, "Oh, wretched creature that spent your days in vanity, you shall continue no longer in the world. And now the wrath of the Almighty is let out upon you."

You are upon your sickbed in distress and your conscience is now awakened and tortures your soul. It tells you that you committed such and such wickedness at such a time, and in such company, and in such a chamber. And now you begin to curse yourself for your folly, for neglecting the day of grace and salvation. Now your time is almost gone. Well, your sickness increases, your pains continue, your friends are all sent for. They come around you bewailing you and you begin to look ghastly and your breath is short. The devil waits for his prey. Your mouth falls, your soul departs, and an end is made of all your vanity and wickedness. This is a picture of the man who has not made God his portion. Mercy has had her time, but you have neglected it and now you are gone forever.

We speak much of the mercy of God, and is it not rich mercy for God to give you such a time of blessed repentance, you wretched, sinful creature, as you have had in this world? For God to call and cry to you and to offer you grace and pardon and peace! He did not do so to the angels that sinned. When they committed just one sin against God, He cast them away and would not even talk with them about any terms of peace. Therefore, seeing that you have had your time already, let all the angels in heaven, all the saints and creatures, yes, and all the devils themselves acknowledge that

God was merciful to this man, to this wretched man and woman who had such a fair time, though judgment is now upon them. Oh, my brethren, the thoughts of death under this notion have a great deal in them to work upon your hearts.

I remember hearing of one who used to pray six times a day and, being asked why he spent so much time praying, he could give no other answer than this, "I must die, I must die." That which was to come after would put a period to the time of his life upon which so much depended. Oh, that we had hearts to consider it, and that we knew even now in our day those things that belong to our everlasting peace before it is too late. Brethren, these things are of infinite concern to your immortal souls. The Lord grant that they may be prevalent upon every one of us.

We may apply this dreadfulness of death (that follows the meditation of this point I have been on) to divers sorts of people. First, I think it should be of great force and efficacy to work upon the hearts of old people. Your time is near. You need to be sure that your work is done, for certainly you do not have long to accomplish that work of making your peace with God. It is three or four o'clock, as it were, in your day of grace. The sun is setting with you. Now if a man is to go on a journey and neglects the forenoon and much of the afternoon, and sees the sun draw low, he thinks to himself, "I must make haste now, for if the sun sets and I am not at my journey's end, I am a lost man. My life is gone."

Men may be able to go over the water where the sea is dry at one time and flows at another, but if they are off by a half an hour they are dead men. If they find that the time is almost come for the waters to return, then their hearts are daunted and they say to one another, "We need to make haste, for the time is almost at an end." Oh, consider this, you old men who have neglected the time of your youth and whose time is almost at an end: know the things of your peace, double now your diligence. It is a most dreadful thing to see an old wicked man, an old sinner, an old scorner, an old carnal wretch, who never understood the great business for which he came into the world.

Secondly, this concerns all profane wretches who, instead of doing the work of their time and preparing for their everlasting estate, go directly backwards and make the breach between God and their souls wider. God has sent you here to live to the praise of His name, and to work out your salvation with fear and trembling, and you have gone directly backwards. The time of your lives has been spent in nothing else but making yourselves seven times more the children of wrath than before. You need to look to yourselves, for if you die in the course of your profaneness, you are undone forever.

Thirdly, for those who have been heretofore in a good forwardness in the way of life and salvation, who have had some stirrings of conscience in them but yet, through the violence of their lusts have been turned back again and have fallen off from the former estate, certainly this point might strike you to the heart. It is like a man who is to go over the sea by such and such a time and has a good gale for the present. But when he has come near the shore, a great gust drives him back again. What a sad condition this man is in! So it is with you. The time was when you had a good gale. God came graciously to you by the work of His Spirit and you seemed to be making progress in the work for which you were born. But the gust of sin and the violence of lust has carried you back again, and now you are further off than before. How should this awaken you to improve all your time and opportunities to the uttermost for the good of your soul.

Also this concerns those who, upon every discontent, wish themselves dead. It is this way with some froward people. If anything crosses them, they immediately wish themselves into the grave. Oh, vain man or woman, do you know what you are doing to wish the time of your life to end? You may meet with another manner of discontent than you will ever meet with here, for after death comes judgment. Amos 5:18 says, *Woe unto you that desire the day of the Lord, to what end is it for you? The day of the Lord is darkness and not light.* So I say, woe to them that, in a froward mood, desire the day of the Lord, which is not a day of light but is likely to be a day of darkness unto them. Instead of giving God the praise of your life, do you wish yourselves dead upon every sullen mood? This is a great dishonor to God's grace and mercy extended to you.

Again, this concerns those who will venture their lives upon every drunken occasion. It is true that fools will venture their lives for trifles because they do not know the worth of them, but those who know the worth of their lives will not do so. I remember a story of a philosopher who was very afraid, being at sea and in danger of his life. The mariners were not at all afraid and said, "Are you afraid, a philosopher, when we rude mariners do not fear?"

He replied, "Aye, and there is a reason for it. If I die, a philosopher is gone; but your lives are not worth as much." So that they are ready to venture their lives in a drunken quarrel and will venture nothing for God. They do not know what their lives are worth, and that is why they are so willing to throw them away.

Also, it concerns those who, in trouble and anguish of conscience, are ready to lay violent hands upon themselves to take their own lives. One would think that this point opened and applied might forever keep back such a temptation for time to come. What an infinite, desperate folly is this that I, who am made aware of God's wrath and am afraid of it, shall yet do that which may put me irrecoverably into it, and seal me eternally in it, as they do who lay violent hands upon themselves. If any people in the world should desire the continuance of their lives and prize them at a high rate, those who are troubled in conscience should do it. They should pray David's prayer of Psalm 39:13, *O spare me, that I may recover strength, before I go hence and be no more.*

Use God's own argument, Psalm 103:13-14, where it is said that God is merciful to His people because He remembers they are just dust. So plead with God and say, "O Lord, spare me. I am just dust, and a wind that passes away and shall never return again. Oh, let my life continue, for if this time is out I am gone forever."

Lastly, this concerns those that have been dying, as they thought, upon their death beds, who have apprehended themselves as dying and have had this truth somewhat settled upon them, who have seen eternity before them and have been in danger, as they conceived, of everlasting ruin. In their own judgments they have received judgment, but God has magnified His mercy towards them and has restored them again. Perhaps in this condition, when you saw and had the judgment in your own heart that your time was gone, you made promises and said, "Oh, if God would spare my life, what a new man I would be! I would be sure to make use of my time in another manner than ever before." Well, God has raised you up again and what then? Now you will venture upon God's patience and His wrath as well. Oh, woe to you when your days are ended and this judgment comes. It will fall dreadfully upon you.

Wherefore, my brethren, let me speak to all of you, for I am not come this day just to spend an hour with you but to do your souls some good. Be it known to you, this is your day, the day of grace and salvation, and yet once again, in the name of God, I declare to you this truth, supposing you have heard it many times before. There is not the worst, the vilest in the congregation who has come through the providence of God but we know it is possible for your sins to be pardoned. It is still possible for your soul to be saved, for God to be reconciled to you, and today it is once again declared to you that you are not yet sealed in eternal misery, which might have been your condition before now.

Oh, that when you have gone home you would get into your closets, fall down before God, and bless Him for this message once again preached to you. Beloved, if I, or any of the servants of the Lord, should be sent by God to the gates of hell with this message, "Oh, you damned spirits, know from the Lord that there is a possibility for you to be saved," they would certainly hearken to such tidings with joyfulness. Now this cannot be preached to them, but this is preached to the vilest, most wicked wretch and enemy to God and goodness that is in this congregation.

God declares this to you now, but how long it will be before judgment comes to seal you in another condition you cannot tell. Therefore know in this, your day, the things of your eternal peace. Who knows what may depend upon one day? Yet prayers and tears may do you some good, but stay awhile, and though streams of blood should flow from you and you should cry and howl to God for all eternity, it would never do it. Therefore, know your time.

It is a happy thing for a man to do business in such a time wherein he may have the benefit of it. Among men, if a thing is done but not in the proper season, it loses its worth and efficacy. So now, prayers, tears, mourning and crying to God for mercy, have no efficacy unless they are done in time. You know that unless they are done this day, or tomorrow, or very shortly, they may do you no good at all. Therefore, take your time. God proclaims and says to every one of you this day, "Poor creature, if you ever expect to receive mercy in the day of Christ, look to it now, for the golden scepter is stretched forth. Now is the acceptable time and the day of grace and salvation. Come in, accept the offers and tenders of grace and mercy now, or else you are gone forever."

Wherefore, then, let this take off all slightness of heart and those roving dispositions of your spirits that run so after vanities. If a man who was wild in his thoughts and had roving eyes should have someone say to him, "Sir, consider what you do, for it concerns your life. If you miscarry, you are a dead man." This would make him call in his thoughts and compose his spirit. So if you have a slight and wandering heart, this is said to you this day, "Friend, poor soul, know what you are doing. Even this day's work concerns all your life, your eternal estate, and take yourselves off from all creatures until you have done so great a work."

So says the Apostle in I Cor. 7:29-32, *Brethren, the time is short, it remaineth that both they that have wives be as if they had none; and they that weep as though they wept not; and they that rejoice as though they rejoiced not; and they that buy as though they possessed not; the time is short.* The word means that the time is wrapped up, the time is all folded up. Therefore, let your hearts be taken off of the creature. Truly, brethren, whatever you think of this point, those who understand themselves rightly would not venture to be in an unconverted state one half hour for ten thousand worlds. They know that when death comes, judgment comes also.

You who are poor people, who hardly live and are in great extremity in this world, as long as you live here, your condition is comfortable, for you have time to do that work which is of such mighty consequence for the good of your souls. Indeed, upon the consideration of this point, people's hearts should be taken off of the creature. A man would be better to live here in order to do that great work, even though it were as a stick or a log in a fire, than to be taken away before he had done the work for which he was sent into the world. When men are in pain they would gladly die, but if they knew what the state and condition of a wicked man will be immediately after his death, they would rather live, even though it was as the most miserable creature in the world.

And consider now, all you young ones, while God gives you time, this great work of making your peace with God. If a man were to go overseas on business of great weight, what should his first thought be after he comes ashore? Let him first make sure of his great work and then be merry later. If you have made sure of this great work, that your peace is made with God and that your everlasting state is secure, then you may be merry among your friends and may live joyfully and comfortably all your days.

It was the complaint of one that art is long and life is short, but surely the art of providing for eternity is a long and difficult art, and your life is short and uncertain. Oh, therefore, do not put off this great work, as Seneca speaks of some who are always <u>about</u> to do something. They are about to live, but they never live. Oh, that you who are young ones would begin soon, and this point settled upon the hearts of young ones would cause them to apply themselves with all their might to the great work of their souls. And that which you do, do it with all your might. This is the argument of the Holy Ghost, Ecc.9:10, *Whatsoever thy hand findeth to do, do it with all thy might; for there is no work, nor device, nor wisdom in the grave whither thou goest.* If you ever had a work to put forth your strength on, do it here. Do not only have some faint wishes and desires, and some sudden good moods as you may have upon hearing some truth such as this. No, but work out your salvation with fear and trembling. Be sure to take hold of all opportunities, seeing so much depends upon the short time of your lives.

If a man were to go overseas and had a fair day and wind, it would be desperate folly for him to say, "Well, I have two or three more days to make the trip, so I will not go now." He neglects this gale, and when those days are passed and the last day comes, he thinks he can go, but he cannot get a wind for all the world. So many think they will repent when they are about to die. Take heed when you have a gale that you do not neglect it for fear it may never come again. Know that if the Lord stirs any of your hearts this day or any other day by His Word, and you neglect it or go to your business, to your shops, to your sensual pleasures and delights, you may hereafter desire to have such a time of the working of God's Spirit again. But if you gave a thousand worlds for it, you could not have it. Therefore, take heed that you do not neglect this great work.

Upon this ground, labor to make sure. If a man has a work to do and does it amiss, he might be able to mend it afterwards. He need not be so exact about it, but if a man knows that once it is gone out of his hands he can never mend it, he will not be careless. He will lay his work to the rule and labor to make all sure. Know that it is so with you about your eternal condition. That which you do in the world must be available forever, you cannot mend it later. If after you see yourselves cast you should say, "Lord, give me more time, and let me come into the world again, and then I will mend this and the other fault for which I was rebuked." God will say, "No, you cannot return to the earth again."

Therefore, it concerns you to make sure of all while you have time. Do not rest upon blind hopes and desperate adventures, but entertain this thought, "What if it should prove otherwise? What if I should miscarry?" This will mightily daunt a man's heart, especially if he knows that, upon his miscarriage, he is undone forever.

Yet further (which is another branch of this exhortation), my brethren, never balk at any way of God for fear of suffering. Be willing to suffer any hardship for God's way.

How does that follow? Thus, if the time of your life is that upon which the sealing of your eternal condition depends, then it concerns you to go through whatever comes your way. For instance, suppose a man were going to such a place and he must be there at such a time. As he rides swiftly through the streets, dogs bark at him (as dogs usually bark at most at those who ride fastest). How little does he regard the barking of the dogs? But if a man rode only for recreation, then it would be troublesome for him.

When a man rides for his life, though the clouds gather and the rains fall, he will not return. If he meets with a foul and dirty way, he will go through it. If he meets with a slough, he will go over it because it is for his life. But if a man is only riding for recreation and meets with winds, clouds, and storms, he will turn back again. Truly, brethren, the ways of most Christians in religion are such as if they took them up for recreation and nothing else. Therefore, if there is only a cloud rising, a little trouble and affliction appearing, they repent their way and turn back again.

Oh, if God would reveal to you what eternity is and what depends upon the course of your life here, then, though there were clouds, storms, tempests, and rugged ways, you will be ready to go through all. The conclusion, therefore, is this: whenever you are tempted to sin, labor to repel temptations by what you have heard today. Say, "God has showed me this day the great errand and business for which I came into the world. He has shown me of what infinite concern those things are that depend upon the time of my life. Shall I, then, satisfy the lusts and corruptions of my own heart, and gratify the devil and the world, and in the meantime neglect that which is of such great importance for the good of my soul?"

Oh, that you knew all the things that concern your eternal peace in this your day! Consider what has been said and the Lord give you understanding hearts to make use of it.

This sermon was preached April 29, 1641.